CULTURE CLASH
DREAD MEETS PUNK ROCKERS

To Nicky → 2009

THE MISSING LINK!

DON LETTS
WITH
DAVID NOBAKHT

S·A·F

CULTURE CLASH
DREAD MEETS PUNK ROCKERS

DON LETTS
WITH
DAVID NOBAKHT

SAF

First published in hardback edition in 2007 by SAF Publishing
This paperback edition first published in 2008

SAF Publishing Ltd.
149 Wakeman Road, London.
NW10 5BH
ENGLAND

email: info@safpublishing.co.uk
www.safpublishing.co.uk

ISBN: 978 0 946719 99 0

Cover and book design: David Nobakht.
Front cover photos: Rocco Redondo, (main photo)
     J.R. (Don Letts)
Back cover photo: Phil Fisk.

In some cases it has not proved possible to ascertain or trace original
illustration copyright holders, and the publishers would be grateful to hear
from the photographers concerned.

The publishers would like to thank 3am Magazine for use of some material.

All lyrics quoted are for review, study or critical purposes.
A CIP catalogue record for this book is available from the British Library.
Printed in England by the Cromwell Press, Trowbridge, Wiltshire.

For

Liberty, Honor, Amber, Jet.

CONTENTS

FOREWORD

*"There weren't that many black punks around during the late seventies.
I used to dream of being a DJ like Don Letts. I loved the way that he
integrated reggae into the punk scene."*

Daddy G (Massive Attack)

In a lot of ways, the title for this book chose itself. The idea of a clash of cultures summarises a man whose life has found him continually balanced between two poles: the predominantly white world of art/fashion, video and film-making in the UK on one side, and the black sensibility of Jamaican reggae, hip-hop and black politics on the other. Few black artists have so successfully managed to unite these disparate elements as has Don Letts.

Letts continually refers to himself as a first-generation British born black, and it is this upbringing that has given him his unique viewpoint. It is a status given to those whose parents came over to England from the West Indies following the Second World War.

Letts' own parents arrived in England from Jamaica in 1955 following the path that the *Windrush* ship had begun when it sailed into Kingston Harbour, Jamaica in May 1948. The ex-Nazi troopship had been captured, refitted and renamed the *Empire Windrush*. The ship's owners advertised in *The*

Gleaner offering tickets for the voyage from Kingston to Britain for twenty-eight pounds and ten pence which, although half the usual fare, was still six months' wages for most West Indians at that time. For some the promise of a new life was too great to ignore and eventually over 500 hopefuls counted their pennies and took advantage of the cheap ticket offer. On the 24th of May, 1948, the *Empire Windrush* left Kingston for Tilbury Docks at the mouth of the Thames.

The *Windrush* stopped briefly in Cuba and Bermuda, where the West Indian passengers got off the ship to stretch their legs. The men, dressed in sharp suits topped with trilby hats, and the women in their sensible coats and smart skirts were deeply shocked to be placed in a 'Blacks Only' enclosure at the cinema they visited whilst there. Segregation was something that they had maybe heard about, but until that point not experienced.

It is often said that if you get more than six Jamaicans together, they will soon turn the event into a party. The *Windrush* was no different; on the Atlantic leg of the passage the ship had three bands and accompanying calypso singers and the parties continued into the night.

HMS Sheffield was shadowing the voyage, as the *Windrush* skipper's cheap ticket offer became public and the unease of the British Government became apparent. Even before the ship reached Britain there were arguments in the Houses of Parliament about whether the passengers should be turned away and sent back to Jamaica—the *Sheffield* was under strict orders to force the *Windrush* to turn-about with its cargo if there was any hint of trouble. (Eventually the British Government decided that if the passengers had British Passports they would be allowed to stay.)

The Britain that lay before those who disembarked was far from the promised land. Food rationing was still a part of daily life. The euphoria at the end of World War II had well and truly fizzled out. Demob happy had given way to Demob fury; a paper shortage, dock workers striking over wages and conditions, doctors and dentists deeply suspicious of the new National Health Service as it threatened to jeopardise their salaries. People in Britain had nothing to spare emotionally or financially, and the hopefuls from the *Windrush* walked straight into the turmoil. Some of the West Indians on board already had a good idea of what they would do once they reached Tilbury Docks. Several of the men would join their compatriots in the RAF, others were already skilled workers and had contacts in Britain waiting to help them out. One guy even bought a ticket to avoid a thirty-five thousand dollar gambling debt.

After the *Windrush* docked, many of the passengers found themselves spending their first nights in Britain at a shelter in Clapham. Had the new arrivals been placed in Kensington or Hampstead, then those areas today would have a significantly different cultural make-up. From Clapham, the new visitors headed for the nearest labour exchange, which was in Brixton. Within days most found work and accommodation in the local area. Almost overnight, Brixton became a multiracial society.

Don's parents—St. Ledger and Valerie Letts—boarded the *Queen Mary* in Kingston, Jamaica and came to Britain in 1955. After two World Wars, Britain was faced with a new world of unstable colonies, economic recession and a severe manpower deficit. Both London Transport and the new National Health Service had canvassed the West Indies looking for enthusiastic workers to fill the labour shortage, and Letts' parents decided that coming to Britain would be a good move. Having grown up in Jamaica under British rule, and being neither radical nor left wing, they had not experienced the negative side of colonialism. Their world really did end at the bottom of their street. Under colonial rule they thought that people were better mannered and better behaved. As Don himself says, "Many of that generation thought that they were being treated well in their new life and thought, 'Well, this is not that bad, as our great-, great-grandfather was cutting sugar in chains.'"

Don's parents, like many others, were blissfully ignorant of what was to come. Had they been more worldly, they would have probably been angrier. (The children of this generation, including Don, would show much more anger toward the prejudice and racial tension they were to experience).

Don's parents' generation had come to Britain with an idealistic vision, but found they had to contend with the miserable British weather as well as racism. Like many, they arrived expecting a promise of integration that did not materialise, so they kept a stiff upper lip throughout a time of race riots, the National Front, political scandals and xenophobic misinformation. The Trades Unions were being pressured by their white members about the numbers of immigrant workers being employed in the nationalised industries. Added to that, workers were being brainwashed by racist right-wing political organisations. These tensions came to a head with the race riots of 1958, in Notting Hill and Nottingham.

All this seems a long way from the sight of a dreadlocked black man DJ-ing in a club full of thrashing white punks, playing dub reggae and rolling spliffs for punters, many experiencing their first cannabis high.

The assimilation of Jamaican culture within the ranks of white youth had actually begun some years earlier through their discovery of Ska and Blue Beat. As Letts says, "Working class British kids had always aligned themselves with black music. Jeannette [Letts early girlfriend] really knew her reggae. She had been listening to the Trojan stuff since she was eleven years old and had been to a few blues parties."

Through his connections, Letts was the reggae expert to the major players on the punk scene. He was largely instrumental in introducing reggae and dub to the suburban kids via the Roxy Club and the fashion shop he managed called Acme Attractions. Whilst John Lydon and Joe Strummer already knew their reggae, it was Letts that introduced them to the latest releases and gave them a deeper insight into Jamaican culture.

"Don had access to many pre-release reggae tunes," recalls Ari Up from the Slits, the all-girl punk band that Letts briefly managed. "I can remember Don had a pre-release copy of 'Uptown Top Ranking' that he played to me. Don's C90 compilation tapes were legendary. He was the original rebel dread. Black people could not pigeon hole him and neither could white. People did not fuck with Don because they could not place him. He was radical and totally open-minded."

For their part, the punks taught Letts an important lesson in DIY; "Just get up and do it!"

As Letts puts it, "As for what I learned from my association with the punks—besides the fact that we became closer by understanding our differences, and not by trying to be the same—well, I learned to make my problems my assets, and that a good idea attempted is better than a bad idea perfected. Punk wasn't just a soundtrack or a uniform that you'd wear for a day. Punk is a frame of mind, an attitude that informs how you do what you do—I picked up a Super-8 camera and reinvented myself as a film-maker."

Don Letts had arrived at the heart of London's punk scene via the small, incestuous fashion world based around Chelsea's King's Road in the early seventies. In 1971, Westwood and McLaren transformed 430 King's Road into something that resembled a living room from a fifties B-movie. This anti-retail experience was called Let It Rock, which became Too Fast To Live Too Young To Die, and soon after that it was shrewdly renamed SEX.

In 1975 SEX took Westwood and McLaren's notoriety to a new level, but a shop located in the basement of a snooty antiques market was giving them a run for their money. Behind the counter of Acme Attractions was a young Don

Letts, with his wraparound shades, leopard-skin waistcoat, dreads and flecked trousers, playing a heavy dub reggae soundtrack.

Phil Strongman worked at Acme for a while and remembers the first time he visited the basement and met Letts.

"I saw this neon red sign with Acme Attractions on it, as I walked down the stairs the dub got louder. There were three or four pictures of black American motorcycle gangs, below them was a picture of Brigitte Bardot and above them was a picture of the Beatles. In middle of the shop was a big red scooter like the one used in the film *Rebel Without A Cause*, and five or six jukeboxes.

"There was Don behind the counter with a spliff in his hand, which was a big deal. You got ninety days for getting caught with a joint then. In those days there was nothing like Acme, with its atmosphere, music and clothes."

As Letts himself attests, "Acme was much more than just a shop. It was a place to hang out; a lifestyle; an attitude. But most of all, it was a forum for talent. At Acme there was a social interaction going on between the different cultures."

It was via this interaction that Letts became resident DJ at the Roxy and started his life as a film-maker.

"The first time I met Don," says Jane Ashley, daughter of Laura Ashley, "he was working at Acme all day and then DJ'ing at the Roxy in the evenings. My first impression was that he was good looking, charismatic and witty. Many women were attracted to him and he had many female friends. He treated everybody the same and did not seem to be impressed by anybody. Don was focused, articulate, ambitious and definitely somebody that was going somewhere."

Letts' status within Punk became similar to that of Pennebaker within the Dylan entourage, or Paul Morrissey to Warhol's Factory starlets. Essentially, the documenter of a scene—a man in the right place, at the right time, with the right attitude, and a camera in hand. Letts' close association with the main players on the punk scene granted him unlimited access and his film *The Punk Rock Movie* captured the raw energy.

Following his departure from the Clash, Mick Jones asked Letts to join his new band, Big Audio Dynamite. B.A.D. painted on a broad canvas and their groundbreaking debut album, *This is Big Audio Dynamite* was instantly well-received.

"B.A.D. were the first to use sampling technology extensively and the way we used samples was unique," says fellow member Dan Donovan. "All Don's samples had meaning and relevance to the tracks they were used on. It was an integral part of the band. We successfully married the organic with the technological."

Letts' work has spanned black and white, film and music, and through his myriad associations he has been instrumental in the assimilation of Jamaican culture into a wider arena. When not behind a camera, Don Letts can still be found DJ'ing his heavy dub soundtrack as the Dub Cartel.

Don and myself have put this book together very much as an oral history. I let him tell his story into a tape recorder, the tape rolling in the same way he allowed the camera to roll in his early films. We then spliced and edited, cut and pasted—hopefully without ever losing Don's voice. Beyond this introduction, I have mostly avoided narrative or explanation, letting Don's unique voice lead you through his life.

David Nobakht

London

1

FUNKY LONDON CHILDHOOD

My earliest memories go back to Brixton. There was myself, my parents and my brothers; Norman, Desmond and Derrick. Desmond was from a previous relationship on my mother's side and Derrick likewise on my father's. I was born in London on the 10th January, 1956. It was the year that Elvis Presley entered the charts with "Heartbreak Hotel", and Hitchcock's *The Man Who Knew Too Much* was showing at the cinema.

My parents had to become Anglicised to get by. It is what that generation tried to do, and as first-generation born blacks we saw that it was not really working out for them. My father worked for London Transport, driving a Routemaster bus, progressing to being a chauffeur for the New Zealand High Commissioner in later years. My mother was a dress-maker.

In my parents' eyes, certain things were just not done. For instance you could not speak disrespectfully—like saying 'no' in the wrong tone, or giving them bad 'looks', and you definitely couldn't 'kiss' your teeth. Any of these transgressions were dealt with swiftly. My mother would hit us with anything that was within easy reach. I still bear a scar on my hand from a bread knife. My mother's expertise lay in a swift and deadly execution of punishment—how just, was another matter.

My father added mental as well as physical punishment to his armoury. If we committed an offence the torture would be signposted with; "Wait till your dad gets home". Depending on what time of day it was, this could fuck with my head—not to mention my underpants. But I must make it clear that the memories of my upbringing are not that of abuse or anything of the kind. Quite the contrary. My parents generation made many sacrifices during their life so that we could have a better one. For bigger crimes, like those spawned by the long summer holidays, either a switch from a tree which grew in the next door neighbours' garden, or dad's belt swung into action. Norman, as the youngest, got it worse 'cause we were older and could lie more convincingly. When we broke the bed by using it as a trampoline—although I was the fattest, and Desmond was bigger than both of us—of course it was little Norman that got blamed. When Desmond broke the kitchen window, we three swore blind that a stone thrown by the 'Greeks' some ten houses away had caused the damage.

My mother is like Mike Tyson in a skirt when she's angry—ask the 'Greeks'. For example, I remember that I was on the receiving end of grief from some skinhead-types and had to make a tactical retreat home. My mother heard them shouting "nigger" this, and "wog" that, in the street and stepped boldly outside, trusty bread knife in hand. The gang did the right thing.

The long summer holidays were an ideal time for the committing of childhood misdemeanours; not that four boys needed much excuse. For example, the time we decided to get rid of the tree that supplied the branches that our young skin was familiar with come punishment time. Inches into the trunk with a tiny hacksaw we realised that the tree would be missed if we managed to hack it down.

"OK, let's make some tree poison," we conspired. A brew of ingredients was picked from the kitchen (which, as all young boys know, is really a science laboratory). Bleach, soap powder, vinegar—anything we could get our hands on—were mixed to a very precise recipe in a large bucket. But just before we poured it onto the tree's roots we realised that if the tree died, questions would be asked, licks would be delivered, tears would roll. So we swiftly aborted the plan and disposed of the poison by throwing it over the wall into next door's garden, and in the process over a bed of sunflowers.

After dinner we heard the wailing of Miss Harris, the gentle old granny-type who was our next-door neighbour. The whole Letts tribe ran into the garden to see what was up. She looked like her world had collapsed. The once towering sunflowers no longer reached for the sky but lay flat against the soil: dead. We, like everyone else, threw our hands up in utter disbelief. After all, we believed our poison was made specifically for trees, not sunflowers.

The episode proved to be a double-disaster for us boys, as the sunflowers supplied the bumblebees around which we used to tie a length of thread and then fly like little kites. When we got bored with that, we'd let them go, only to watch them fly off into the overhead telephone cables where they flew around and around in decreasing circles to eventually die trapped by the pieces of thread. We also heated the bottom of empty milk bottles on the Bunsen Burner—sorry make that the kitchen stove—and dropped spiders in them to watch them 'dance or die'.

It's paradoxical, 'cause as a child I basically loved animals and insects. In my time I've kept frogs, cats, dogs, terrapins, newts, rabbits, hamsters, mice and gerbils.

Basically if it could fit in a cage I owned one. I remember trying to teach the mice to swim, only for them to drown five minutes later. Trixie the dog was taken in the family car and released in the area of Battersea Dogs Home, for continually using my leg as a sex aid while we gathered together for our evening meal. Once, on an archaeological dig in our backyard I made a unique find of some really well-preserved bones only to be told by my father that I'd just desecrated the unmarked grave of my pet rabbit.

Two other incidents from my early childhood were to leave a deep impact on me. One for more obvious reasons than the other. During yet another school summer holiday Desmond, Norman and myself decided to play *Batman*. Now if there was ever a really stupid thing to do Norman was usually first in line as the youngest. But on this occasion it was somehow decided that I would be the one to jump out of our third story bedroom window. Unfortunately Fatman couldn't hold on to the rope that was too thin in the first place. I must have hit the ground at 60 m.p.h. with severe rope burns to both hands.

The other was the time me, Norman and 'Cherry Nose' (a neighbourhood friend) went swimming at the local open-air pool. An innocent enough idea, except none of us could swim. We're daring each other to see who can jump in the pool the furthest and make it back to the edge. Must have been that extra weight! Once again it's me that's watching my life flash before me as I'm flailing around out of my depth and drowning, quite literally. The next thing I remember is having my chest pumped by a white guy on the edge of the pool. How I survived those summer holidays I'll never know.

2

WHAT'S HAPPENING BROTHER?

I really don't remember much about my eldest brother Derrick. If my memory serves me well, he came over from Jamaica
not long after my parents settled, if not immediately. He was
already into his troublesome teens and the inevitable generation clash occurred. Since we were considerably younger,
there was little interaction between Derrick and the rest of
us. This situation was further polarised by the 'ism's' and
'schism's' of being a black teenager in an alien culture. All I
remember of Derrick was a lot of grief between my parents as
he went through a kind of sex, drugs and rock'n'roll rights-of-
passage—or at least the sixties black equivalent.

   He was the first one to introduce me to the concept of
"style"; part of his 'rebellion' was his adoption of the fashion
statements of the time; mohair suits, white roll-necks, dark
glasses, all backed by an Otis Redding soundtrack. A kind
of 'rude boy'. He looked like one of the few black guys who

appeared on *Ready Steady Go*. It wasn't long before he became a regular at the Ram Jam club on Brixton Road. It was *the* place to be, Geno Washington and the Ram-Jam Band was the resident entertainment. Derrick also introduced me to the delights of international cuisine. To a working-class kid chow-mein from the local Chinese take-away was pure exotica.

Derrick hung out with the other local teenagers, who all looked equally undesirable to the prudish Jamaican parents who were careful to tow the line in their new homeland. My parents had framed pictures of the Queen in our living-room. My generation was better educated and had a more worldly view, and there was no way we could follow them down that path. We thought, "Hang on, we have got fuck all to be grateful for." Perhaps they were a little envious of a new black British generation who were trying to find their own place in the world and create their own reality. Consequently late-night shouting matches with Derrick about clubbing, or about the 'type' of girls he was hanging with were the first signs. Locking him out when he missed a curfew soon led to, "If you think you're a man now you can find somewhere else to live". At eighteen years of age Derrick did. My father used that line two more times in his life.

My mother never seemed to really accept Derrick as her own. Because he actually wasn't. I'm sure this all took its toll. Derrick really never stood a chance, poor bastard. He was the first womanising playboy in my family; at least to my then limited knowledge. Although he never left London, I had no idea where he lived, and we have accidentally bumped into each other about five times over the last twenty years. However the recent death of my father changed that, and we've begun to form a relationship again.

Desmond—now there's a character. Being from a previous relationship on my mother's side, Desmond also suffered from a lack of understanding from my father. Like Derrick he too was brought to the promised land to suffer a very similar fate. But since Desmond was much closer in age to me and Norman, we consequently spent more time together. His real father was a womanising gambler. Are there genes for these traits? He would take me and Norman to the local comic shop and liberate the latest DC comics, and guess who carried the bags? I would have been about nine, Norman a few years younger and Desmond about thirteen. Having said that, I don't really know anybody's age in my family, nor anyone's birthday.

There's a reason my family is so fragmented and I believe my mother to be the protagonist. When Desmond was about fourteen he got into some trouble for shoplifting with some friends in the West End. Since they were all juveniles, the police let them off with a scolding. My mother was so incensed by the fact that Desmond had caused her the unbearable shame of the police knocking on our front door—and in front of the neighbours too—that she told the police she didn't want him back. Desmond was shipped off to a home and my mother didn't speak to him for about five years.

However before he was exiled he had plenty of time to abuse and use us two 'stooges' with a charm that was to serve him well in later years. He used to lock Norman and me in a cupboard when we pissed him off. Since he was the oldest he had to look after us while my parents worked. Consequently Norman and I spent a lot of time in that cupboard.

In those days us boys all shared one room, the toilet was outdoors and seemed miles away, especially in the winter. To relieve ourselves, we had a communal piss-pot which became dangerously full by morning. Since Norman and I were the smallest, the deadly task of emptying the chamber pot was left to the more responsible Derrick and Desmond. The task was bad enough when Derrick was around (more people, more piss), but since he'd gone it was Des's duty to negotiate the two flights of stairs each morning. It was only a matter of time. It was the loose carpet on the stairs. I doubt Desmond will ever forget being drenched in urine that had been left to brew overnight.

We had no indoor bath. In summer, Norman and I would wash in an old zinc bath in the garden. This was a source of great entertainment to the 'Greeks' ugly daughters and even greater embarrassment to us. Now I come to think of it, I never saw my parents in that old zinc bath. Later on it became Desmond's duty to escort us to the public bathhouse in Camberwell every Saturday night. A peculiar place, the very thought of which makes me shudder. You had to holler, "More hot in number four," when you needed more water. Of course Des decided it was more economic if Norman and I shared. But anything was better than hearing the sniggering ugly Greek girls.

Times had changed and Desmond's soundtrack was Hendrix, Sly Stone, and later on, Funkadelic. Des had got a job in a Carnaby Street record shop, which in those days was a gateway to a world most people could only read about. And the sign above the door read: SEX, DRUGS AND ROCK'N'ROLL in great big letters. Des now had a foot in this door, and I was his brother.

Over the years, and since the death of my father St. Ledger, my mother's attitude has softened somewhat. Her sons are now all in communication with her and each other. I have come to realise that her hard exterior was a protective device. Life must have been incredibly difficult for my parents' generation—strangers in a strange land.

3

OLD SCHOOL

Christchurch Primary was a mixed school where I passed from laddish indifference to girls, through to the first stirrings that these curious beings might actually serve some purpose beyond 'kiss chase'. Linda Ward was the love of my life but she was never to know it. It was Christine and Jennifer that gave us our first 'sticky fingers'. A predominately white, Church of England establishment, it was the better of two local schools, the other was Cowley where the roughnecks went. The neighbourhood I grew up in had a liberal sprinkling of Jamaicans, Irish, English and the aforementioned Greeks. As I remember it was about as harmonious as a bunch of displaced misfits could get.

If there was any trouble it was of the type of drama reminiscent of cheap daytime soap operas. I never saw any direct racial trouble. Although when things erupted, as they inevitably would in this fragile ecosystem, people were quick to revert to basic colour-coded insults. We had the usual assortment of urban bit players and everyone knew who the major characters were, and who had bit parts.

I've come to appreciate in later years the sense of community we had in those days. Everyone was aware of their neighbours, there was an unspoken code of ethics. If someone's house was burgled everyone else would notice if X had suddenly acquired a new colour TV. If there was a local villain everybody knew. When the tower block/council estate years came these communities were broken and scattered about. Nowadays you're lucky if you know the name of the man next door. Undesirables move about with anonymity, the results are self-evident—good for some, bad for others.

Unlike the rest of the kids, I never really took part in many of the street activities, preferring to potter about in my 'laboratory' or exploring the possibilities of our garden. I say garden, but it was really a ten-foot square patch of dirt which happened to be attached to our house. I quickly learned that necessity really is the mother of invention, as this was where I tested whatever contraption I'd put my mind to experimenting with. The building of a tree house without a tree comes to mind, along with the attempted launch of the first insects in space.

Occasionally I would venture out onto the street to test my inventions in front of an audience. The local kids would stop playing 'penny up the wall' and gather round to see what I was up to. These displays were usually reserved for things that were likely to explode. Even back then I had a sense of occasion. It might sound like I was the local nerd or something, but I did the street thing too (everything except football and cricket—well actually rule out *all* sports).

At Christchurch Primary my best friend was a white guy called Jeffrey Love. We swore allegiance till the end of time. As it happens it was till the end of term. Robert Culp and Bill Cosby in *I Spy* were our role models, me being the bespectacled brains to Jeffrey's playboy. Man we were stupid.

During the late sixties, I moved on to Archbishop Tennison's School in Oval, south east London. I was truly dropped in the deep end being the only West Indian pupil at the school over a five-year period. My father was so proud when he found out that I'd been accepted by a Grammar School, he ran out and got me a shiny tan leather briefcase with my initials embossed in gold on the side. I hated that briefcase.

We had to wear short trousers for the first year of Grammar School. On the very first day the school bully greeted us 'first years' by slashing our legs with his steel comb. When he made a move on me I smacked him in the mouth—simultaneously the bell for break rang, giving him no time to retaliate. Perfect timing. It wasn't that I was particularly good at fighting, it was just that if I had gone home and told my parents that I'd let someone do that to me they would have beaten me! This saved my arse a few times. The school bully didn't fuck with me any more for one thing. By the same token if I went home and told my parents I'd got a beating from a teacher I'd get a beating from them too.

Whilst at school, I can remember all too well Enoch Powell's 'Rivers of Blood' speech that he made in 1968. He demanded an immediate lowering of the numbers of immigrants setting up life in the UK and wanted those that were already living here to be sent back home. Powell did nothing but stir up racial hatred, and eventually the speech got him sacked from Edward Heath's Shadow Cabinet.

In the middle of the playground there was a flag pole, and one day a kid called 'Horse' was swinging around on the rope used to hoist the flag, when suddenly the flagpole broke from its moorings and began to fall.

In slow motion: school kids scattering for cover... close up: innocent looking blonde-haired 'first year' looks up... cut to: flag pole slicing through the air... mid-shot: pole hits kid on head (sound FX)... pull back to reveal wide shot: kid falls to the ground a river of blood covers an impossibly big area... fade to black. I'd passed out momentarily. How could all that blood come out of one person, and so fast? Amazingly the kid survived. It made the daily papers I think.

I really despised the geography teacher, Mr. Trevelyan. All teachers used to clip kids round the ear, or smack 'em upside the head with a ruler, and usually it was harmless enough—except when that pock-faced bastard Trevelyan did it. He mastered both methods of punishment into feats of Olympic proportions. Every time he made one of my friends cry, I swore vengeance.

One day I'm in the washrooms when in walks Pock-face. Coldly I stare into his eyes, (cue *The Good, The Bad and the Ugly* theme) without blinking I kick one of the wall-to-ceiling mirrors with my brogues customised with Blakeys. The wall of glass lies shattered at my feet. Pock-face can't believe his eyes, he thinks he's got me now. Dragged in by my collar I hang my head in front of the headmaster. Pock-face goes into his rant, the headmaster looks at me for a response.

"Headmaster," I began, "I know I haven't been a model pupil, but do you honestly think I would do something so stupid? It was simply an accident," I said looking into Pock-face's eyes. "The floor was wet causing me to slip breaking the mirror."

That was my version of revenge.

Sometimes when I was bored, or when I felt I was being ignored, I'd do stupid things like setting my desk on fire. Being the only black kid in my school would have been enough to faze most people, 'cause there ain't anything as venomous or cruel as children. Wog, nigger, Kit-E-Kat eater, Brillo bonce, coon, sunshine, chief, sambo—all these names and more were used to try to humiliate me. Whenever they called me a name, I'd proudly reply, "That's right." It was "say it loud, I'm black and I'm proud" as James Brown put it. This would piss them off no end, I even went as far calling my posse Chalky White and the Invincibles. We'd protect the new 'first years' in return for their 'afters'—that's what we called the desserts at school dinners.

My posse included 'Millsy' and 'Froggy', Kim Hewitt and another guy called Chris Arkle. Froggy was my best friend throughout Secondary School—yes, the same old blood-brother-till-death-do-us-part shit—which was actually con-summated by the drawing of blood. Needless to say I don't even know if he's alive now, but back in the day me and him were tight. He was the one that got me hooked on the Beatles. I'd bought "Penny Lane" for seven shillings and six pence, a huge commitment in those days. It was Froggy that taught me the meaning of 'obsession'. Luckily my steadily growing ego would save me from the one-way street of 'fandom', but not before I had acquired the second largest collection of Beatles' memorabilia in England. Froggy and I were 'Apple Scruffs', we'd hang about the Beatles' offices in Saville Row on Saturdays hoping (in vain) to catch a glimpse of the Fab Four. We even managed to blag our way in once and stole some stuff.

Years later in my capacity as a video director I actually ended up not only directing Paul McCartney in the video for Bob Marley's 'One Love' we actually end up 'singing' a chorus together in the clip. Even stranger: the night before John Lennon died, my friend the photographer Bob Gruen, had lent John my show-reel as he wanted to see my work. In the confusion of that fateful evening Bob got access to the Dakota building because he remembered that John said he'd leave my reel with the doorman for him to collect, which he had.

At the age of twelve I had to decide which subjects to pursue to examination level. Simple, right? Wrong. My parents believed that a black person couldn't possibly make a living as an artist. So in my best interests they decided that I should take up physics, chemistry and technical drawing. Years later when it came time to sit my exams, in a moment of rebellion, I wrote on my chemistry paper, "a chemist I was not to be, that I clearly state, 'cause I got a splitting headache and I cannot concentrate."

Were logarithms or the linear coefficient of expansion really gonna help me survive out there? (I've never even heard either mentioned again in a quarter of a century). The hours, days and years they wasted trying to teach totally useless shit was criminal. I drew a nude woman for my technical drawing examination with the caption: "curves are better than straight lines." And anyway, we'd just discovered sex, drugs and rock'n'roll for Christ's sake! God knows what a distraction that can be for a jaded adult, let alone those juveniles who considered they were boldly going were no man had been before.

According to all the education I received at school, my history began with slavery; no black man ever discovered, built or invented anything. Which was complete bullshit. What about the sculptures and carvings of the city of Benin in Nigeria, or the great 'lost' city of Zimbabwe in Southern Africa? Both were there before any European explorer discovered them. Furthermore, the accepted image of perfection— a white, blue-eyed, blonde-haired Jesus—was something I could never achieve no matter how many O-levels I passed. So why try? The white kids were never short of heroes. If I was never shown real examples of what I could achieve, what could I aspire to?

For a real insight into how we were perceived in those days you only have to look at the popular TV of the time; Alf Garnett's *'Til Death Do Us Part*, *The Black and White Minstrel Show* and Jim Davidson's 'Chalky White' comedy routine. That's entertainment.

When I was growing up I thought this was a normal state of affairs. I only came to realise I was different when there was a problem (like Powell's speech) and people reverted to colour-related insults. At school I was taught about the abolition of slavery, but the key role that slavery played in the British economy during the Eighteenth century was too embarrassing to be included on the curriculum. The majority of slaves were in the Caribbean and North America, but some came to Britain and eventually married native-born Britons. There must be quite a few people out there whose great- great-grandfather was in fact an African slave.

In my formative years I was also immersed in white culture. I got to hear things like Captain Beefheart's *Trout Mask Replica* and Cream's *Disraeli Gears*. I had that coming in one ear, and in the other ear I was listening to black music. Being immersed in black and white cultures made me open-minded and was the beginning of me not wanting to be defined by my colour. I did not understand the attitude or school of thought that dictated, "If you are black, then you could only listen to black music and be immersed in black culture." The juxtaposition of black and white cultures side-by-side made things more interesting for me.

4

TROJAN EXPLOSION

My father ran a sound system of sorts, but it was not the kind of sound system that people know today. It was a means for the immigrants to come together after church to exchange news and find out what was happening back home in Jamaica. For Jamaicans, music was an integral part of their day-to-day life, and not just something the kids did, as was horse racing. My father was named Saint Ledger after the famous horse race. His sound system was called 'Duke Letts Superstonic'. Back in Jamaica, on Sundays after church, my father had hired 16mm films and showed musicals to the locals at outdoor venues.

My dad always used to play an album called *Fire Corner* by King Stitt released by Trojan in 1969. Trojan provided my first soundtrack and a musical map where I could trace my roots. British blacks—black British, easy to say now but in those days this was a confusing concept—trust me. The sounds of Trojan struck an understandable chord for the lost tribe growing up in England with a confused duality, and its impact was crucial. I was fourteen in 1970, a rude boy, an Anglicised version of the Jamaican real deal and part of the first generation of British-born blacks.

It was during the Sixties that the Jamaican recording scene became established and the post-colonial optimism in Jamaica reflected a new sound from the recording studios. That new sound was Ska. I could probably fill the rest of this book with the names of all the people who have said that they invented Ska in '59, '60 or '61. The most likely candidate was an employee of Clement Dodd called Cecil Campbell, better known to you and I as Prince Buster. It was Prince Buster who told his guitarist to accentuate the offbeat that created that unique 'chug' sound that powered the sound of Ska.

Ska fitted in perfectly with the mood after Jamaica gained independence in 1962. The music was made by the people, for the people and it had a good time feel to it. The records were made primarily for sound systems, rather than for commercial use. By the time the acetates wore out they had already been replaced with something new. Fierce rivalry soon built resulting in feuds between the recording artists and the producers. Royalties were not paid to the musicians, they would get paid a flat fee of maybe $10 to $20 dollars to record a track. So all these musicians went in and knocked out as many tracks as they could. It was quantity rather than quality, but these guys had to eat and survive in the harsh Kingston ghettos.

Ska was quickly embraced by the Jamaican immigrants in Britain. By 1963 it had leaked out of the Ladbroke Grove shebeens and was becoming one of the country's most popular underground sounds. Back in Jamaica however, Ska had already dominated the culture for half a decade, and by the mid sixties the people and musicians wanted something new. That change would be Rocksteady.

One of the reasons that Ska evolved into the slower tempo of Rocksteady was due to the social climate, although it is said that a particularly hot summer was also partly responsible for slowing down the groove. At the start of the sixties there was a measurable increase in tension and violence in Kingston's dancehalls. The rude boys were Jamaican youths who had come to Kingston after independence, hoping to better themselves and found nothing. Consequently they became outsiders and turned to crime to survive, whether on their own or with their street gangs. I have always said that the people that are good in Jamaica are very good and the people that are bad, WATCH OUT!

The arrival of the rude boy came to play a part in this musical evolution. Rocksteady's characteristic slower rhythm meant dance moves were slower and people were more rooted to the spot and therefore more aware of what was going on around them. The change in tempo also reflected the mood in Jamaica. Following independence in '62, the party was now over and there was a political and social hangover to deal with.

The mighty Trojan Records started out in July '67. The name Trojan was taken from the trucks that Reid used for carrying his sound system. The label went balls-up after a few releases, but in 1968, Lee Gopthal's company, Beat &

Commercial, merged with Island and the label was running again. This time they concentrated on British artists as well as Jamaican. They featured British producers like Dandy and Joe Mansano, as well as their Jamaican counterparts Duke Reid, Lee Perry, Bunny Lee and Clancy Eccles. Subsidiary labels such as Amalgamated, High Note and Lee Perry's Upsetter were soon formed.

In those days it was strictly vinyl 45s, LPs were too risky. Albums would need to be all killer and no filler before punters would part with their hard-earned cash. Trojan was ghetto-wise and released the *Tighten Up* compilations which I picked up on in 1970 at the age of fourteen—as did the skinheads. These compilations featured the best singles, and *Tighten Up Volume 2* came with that risqué artwork that pleased most male teenagers like myself.

It was around this time in my local youth club, The Landsdowne in Stockwell that I first experienced that teen-age love thang. Gina Pascal was her name and to my mind she was the most beautiful thing that walked the earth. She'll never know what an inspiration she was to an overweight four-eyed black kid, hell I'm only realizing it now. This Mauritian beauty was my first muse before I knew what a muse was. You see I had to get my shit together to get the girl!

It's extraordinary to think that this music ended up being the soundtrack to a particular period in British sub-culture. That was the thing about Trojan: the tunes dealt with themes that the youth on the street—both black and white—could identify with. Well, the youth on my street anyway. At a time when there were more summers in front of me than behind, we met in the local youth clubs united on the dancefloor by these very tunes. With unbelievably infectious radio-friendly melodies it was not surprising that Trojan scored a fair few top thirty hits in those days.

Trojan also provided a soundtrack for a new UK tribe, the skinheads, who were predominantly white working class youth that did not give the time of day for any of that hippy stuff. But they did latch onto the Ska and Trojan boom, snapping up the *Tighten Up* series, helping to propel the singles into the charts.

There was a radical difference between the fashion statement skinheads of the sixties and the overtly racist skinhead movement of the late seventies. Many of the sixties skinheads were growing up within multicultural areas. Paul Simonon was one of them. The relationship between skinheads and West Indians was a strange one. They aligned themselves with Trojan music, adopting it as their own, and black culture was a definite influence on certain elements of their dress code, like the West Indian style of suits, narrow hitched-up trousers and Trilby hats. They combined these with Dr Marten boots and braces, which were strictly working-class attire and there was also an Americana influence with the penny loafers and Harrington jackets.

The *Tighten Up* series left a big impression on me and my mates, Trojan was totally anti-establishment with the soundbite lyrics and emphasis on style. I can remember walking around the streets of London around 1970-71 in my Crombie coat; brogue shoes; Levi's Sta-Prest and Ben Sherman shirt—

and those of us who could not afford Ben Sherman had to make do with Brutus.

In fact my respect for Trojan is still there; twenty years later when I was in Big Audio Dynamite, we named our third album *Tighten Up Vol. '88* in honour of those compilations. And in 2003 I put together a compilation for Trojan titled *The Mighty Trojan Sound* which featured tracks I had grown up listening to by John Holt, Big Youth, I-Roy and Dennis Brown to name a few.

By the close of 1968 a new wave of producers spearheaded by such luminaries as Lee 'Scratch' Perry, Bunny Lee and King Tubby pioneered a new sound that would take the music world by storm. Reggae was slower than rocksteady and a product of multi-track tape machines coming into the equation. Trojan Records continued to import Jamaican tunes to the UK scoring hits with Ken Boothe, John Holt and a host of others. On the back of this some even dubbed Studio One as "Jamaica's Motown" at that time. Who would have guessed that an island that itself was the product of colonialism would end up culturally colonising the world with this new sound and its attitude?

5

POWER TO THE PEOPLE

"Black Panther Party members care about the survival of black people, even at the risk of being made political prisoners, or getting killed and murdered by the fascist cops, or being forced into exile."
Bobby Seale, Seize the Time, 1970.

At the start of the seventies I was soul searching, trying to find myself. The "Free Angela Davis" affair was headline news in the States and I was looking forward to my first UK Black Panther meeting in the local community hall. I had proudly read Bobby Seale's *Seize the Time* and Eldridge Cleaver's *Soul On Ice* and wanted to know more. The former was essential reading if you wanted to become more politically aware, and the Black Panthers were the only thing on offer. I also read George Jackson's prison diaries *Soledad Brother*, and *Blood in my Eye*, completed only days before he was killed in San Quentin prison, allegedly attempting to escape. They were powerful and empowering books.

In the UK, the whole Black Panther Party ethos seemed quite alluring. Black people were not taking any shit and at the same time looking really cool with their leather jackets, Afro's and shades. The mixture of soul music and militant right-on politics was a powerful combination.

Doctor Martin Luther King did not encourage violence. But after his assassination in 1968, the Black Panther Party came to the fore and they were prepared to kick ass. Founded by Huey P Newton and Bobby Seale in Oakland, California the Black Panthers' aim was to further promote black liberation for which the Civil Rights Movement, Malcolm X and Martin Luther King had laid the foundations. The Black Panthers rejected the non-violent stance of Doctor King and believed in not compromising with the establishment. The BPP were responsible for free medical treatment, and their "Free Breakfast for Children Program" organised from a San Francisco church fed thousands of hungry children. They gave out clothing and arranged classes on politics, economics and self-defence, as well as striving to end drug use in the African American community by disrupting the operations of drug dealers.

The Angela Davis trial kicked off in 1972 and I followed it as much as I could. Thousands marched in her support in Paris, and in London there were pickets outside the American Embassy. Davis had experienced the racism of the Ku Klux Klan whilst growing up in Birmingham, Alabama and had joined the BPP early on. In 1970 three black prisoners were shot dead in the exercise yard of Soledad Prison by a prison guard. After the verdict of 'Justifiable Homicide' was announced, the prisoners rioted and a white prison guard was killed. Three prisoners were arrested for the murder and were all given the death sentence. They came to be known as the Soledad Brothers. George Jackson was one of them; and his brother Jonathan hatched a plot to kidnap the Judge and take hostages in the Court House. The outcome was that Jackson and the Judge were killed during a shoot out with the police. Angela Davis was accused of providing Jonathan Jackson with firearms, conspiracy to murder and kidnapping. After 49 days in court she was found not guilty. As for George Jackson, he was shot dead during what was reported as an escape attempt from prison.

Having been through the civil rights movement, black Americans never really bought into the idea of a multicultural society. They say there is an equation between getting your arse kicked and getting your shit together. American blacks were forced to get their shit together. They had to deal with motherfuckers running around with white sheets over their heads hanging black brothers and setting them on fire. The legacy is that there is a now a black infrastructure in the US that is economic, intellectual and artistic. It has all those bases covered.

Over here in the UK we had institutionalised racism, but not legislated racism—much more difficult to tie down. So there I was, an alienated first-generation black British youth, and it was no wonder I looked to the American blueprint. But the social development of black America did not really apply to the UK, the difference being their forefathers had been dragged there kicking and screaming, whilst my parents had willingly bought a ticket to come to this country from Jamaica.

If in this country there had been something like the KKK kicking our arse, maybe we would have gone a lot further. Having said that, we had the legacy of Mosley's Blackshirts and I can remember seeing KBW (Keep Britain White) painted on the walls after Enoch Powell made his "rivers of blood" speech.

From reading *Seize the Time* and studying the politics of the Black Panther Party, I gleaned little bits that definitely helped me get through my day; it was empowering and made me feel less isolated. Also James Brown's "Say it loud, I am black and I am proud", simplistic as it is now, was almost a mind-blowing concept. Before that, it was "Don't say I am black" as if it made you a second rate citizen.

So, I got on the bus and went to Oval House where the first UK Black Panther meeting was being held. I can remember listening to the speaker, and next minute I was wondering why everyone was looking down at me. And why was I floating six inches above the ground? Apparently I'd fainted and came to as I was unceremoniously being carried out of the hall. It must have been the 'too big to handle' spliff I had before I got there.

6

HIP TEENS 'N' BLUE JEANS

I left home at sixteen and rented a flat in Wandsworth with a bunch of mates from school. It was an arrangement that didn't last for long, as we continually had arguments about who should do the washing up (the same thing that fucked the hippy movement). So I moved in with my brother Desmond, who was living in a big house in the Whitehorse, Brixton, where I had the attic room for a few years until the Council compulsorily purchased the house.

At the start of the seventies there were a lot of Irish people living in the area and despite all the "Keep Britain White" shit, people of different races basically got on. Things would kick off between neighbours about parking spaces and stuff like that, but in Brixton it was never racial; we were all working class people and we managed to work things out. At the dole office there wasn't a white or a black queue—the realisation came to us that we were all in the same boat. However it was a different matter between the people, the police and the establishment.

I found myself wandering the streets looking for work in 1972 after leaving school. That year the Race Relations at Work section was added to the Race Relations Act, not that it made any difference to me. My world revolved around Marvin Gaye's *What's Goin' On*, Curtis Mayfield's *Superfly* and Isaac Hayes' *Hot Buttered Soul*. I had the Afro with a long blade comb sticking out of it, the dance moves and the look.

Anyone who wanted to go to the best and hippest places for clothes in London would go straight to the King's Road in Chelsea. It was Mary Quant with the opening of Bazaar in 1955 that put Chelsea, and the King's Road in particular, on the fashion map. Fashion has always been a big part of working class lifestyle. It is all about trying to find an identity. For young people clothes, fashion and music went hand in hand. I never followed when it came to fashion, I led. It had its problems later on, walking around Brixton in leather trousers whilst my brethren looked at me in total shock—without the awe.

In the sixties Granny Takes A Trip dressed the stars. The Beatles could be seen wearing Granny's shirts on back of the *Revolver* sleeve and the Rolling Stones also wore attire from the shop as seen on the sleeve of *Between the Buttons*. Early Pink Floyd were also heavily into Granny's clothes, and their fashion became an integral part of their stage show with their regular performances at the UFO club in Tottenham Court Road.

A few doors down from Granny's, at 430 King's Road, was Hung On You that sold kaftans and items of ethnic clothing. Hung On You later became Mr Freedom. Tommy Roberts' and Trevor Miles' Mr Freedom was like being in a giant play area for kids, with a stuffed blue gorilla, a revolving silver globe hanging from the ceiling and jars of sweets behind the counter. The clothes were influenced by over-the-top fifties fashion and Hollywood. The shop was full of pop-art items like Mickey Mouse T-shirts, Superman jackets and fake leopard-skin everywhere. Amongst Mr Freedom's customers were Peter Sellers and Mick Jagger. Malcolm Edwards, later known as Malcolm McLaren, could also be seen browsing.

After a while Miles found that his clothes and ideas were being ripped off, most notably the extremely successful star T-shirt that he had designed. When Tommy Roberts split to set up another shop elsewhere, Miles rechristened Mr Freedom as Paradise Garage, opting for a different look that could be defined as 'Pacific Exotic'. There was an Americana feel to Paradise Garage, as he had imported Hawaiian shirts and used jeans from New York. Miles soon found that he was facing serious competition from established places like Granny Takes A Trip, as well as newer upstarts like Alkasura that sold crushed velvet clothing to rock stars like Marc Bolan.

When Trevor Miles went off on his honeymoon he was oblivious to the fact that the manager he left in charge had rented out some of Paradise Garage's shop space to Malcolm McLaren and Vivienne Westwood who promptly set up Let

It Rock. They started by selling fifties records and clothes and soon they had taken over the whole shop.

At that time not only the retro-looking Teddy Boys were interested in fifties clothing, the fashion elite were as well. The whole look was epitomised by Bryan Ferry and the early Roxy Music albums. Let It Rock was the only place that sold brothel creepers, as well as hound's-tooth drapes with velvet collars and mohair jumpers. On a typical day there was an assortment of drag queens, Teddy Boys and people like sculptor Andrew Logan buying the clothes. What Let It Rock did was give fifties fashion an authentic street edge. Vivienne Westwood still has a shop at 430 King's Road today.

I have always recognised the limitations of fashion. Instead of spending time developing a fashion sense, I spent a lot more time developing my common sense. I realised that having one without the other just made you a clothes horse. Not only did I look fucking good, I had my shit together. A lot of people might view this as arrogance, but the clothes were not my armour, my character was.

There has always been an element of looking smart in Jamaican culture. Look at the pictures of the *Windrush* generation coming off the ship, they were not wearing loin cloths or sacks, the men were wearing smartly tailored suits with Trilby hats and the women looked pretty damn smart in their coats and dresses too. My parents retained this ethic; I was always sent to school looking very sharp.

I spent a lot of time browsing in the King's Road, and was immediately attracted to the lifestyle of the people working there, so it was only a matter of time before I got a job briefly at Oggi E Domani, a high fashion, Italian designer boutique similar to the early-seventies L'Uomo Vogue style. Working there sucked, I was really talked down to, so I left to work for Jean Machine. My relationship with my parents was not great at this time. Having sent me to grammar school, I was now working in a clothes shop on the King's Road and they saw me as a failure.

It is hard to believe it now, but for a brief period of time the Jean Machine chain was the hippest place to work in London. It was *the* alternative before Punk Rock. The hippies did not have that much appeal as they were styleless. Jean Machine was where all the sex, drugs and rock'n'roll was happening.

All the staff in Jean Machine, and its customers, wanted to be Warhol stars—characters like Andrew Logan and Piggy, Luciana and Michael and Golinda, who had all emerged from the Biba/ glam rock/ Bowie scene. They were all freaks in their own right. I particularly remember a six-foot blonde Monroe lookalike called Wendy. I was the young whippersnapper, as I had come up from South London, whereas all the other staff came from Chelsea and Kensington. The management hired only what they considered to be 'the beautiful people'—not just in looks but also in attitude. Loud queens, obvious dykes, part-time trannies, and me black and confident. Or maybe it was just that they wanted someone with an Afro to complete the cast. I became acutely aware that amongst the beautiful people my colour was not only in vogue but very much an asset.

This was a fascination which can be traced back through time—an interest in the exotic, the dark, the dangerous door to the city of spades, the forbidden world of big cocks, cool drugs combined with the best soundtrack. 'Brown sugar how come you taste so good?' It's all bullshit really.

These were truly great times and the perfect place to further my education. Arguably better than the sixties, since it was less naive, there was none of that 'make love not war' slogan shit, we came to party, and in between partying we sold jeans and were paid a commission. This meant we had to become masters of bullshit to sell as many jeans as possible. Money was never a problem for me back then. There seemed to be a never-ending stream of women needing a hand to get into jeans that were a size too small. We had a technique to help do the zips up, which entailed lying the female customers on the floor. After such intimacy getting their phone number was a cinch.

A lot of popular subculture back then was kick-started out of boutiques. The gay scene was very much a part of Jean Machine culture. There was a club that I used to go to called Sombreros on High Street Kensington; Bowie used to pop in there a few times. The scene was very hedonistic and devoid of politics—in an odd sort of way a politic in itself. There were some hippy ideals there but it was a lot more fashion-orientated. At that time I was moving between the L'Uomo Vogue crowd and the beautiful freaks at Jean Machine. All my life I have constantly moved between things, never following the herd or being trapped by one genre. It is not something that I think about, it is the way I am.

7

YOU'RE GONNA
WAKE UP ONE MORNING

In an atmosphere of IRA bombs going off in London, racism and the rise of the National Front, Chelsea continued to be a melting pot of fashion and counter culture. I remember one day in the early seventies, I was walking up the King's Road and came across Let It Rock. It was like an Aladdin's cave of subculture. Then, in 1973 Let It Rock mutated into Too Fast To Live Too Young To Die, selling biker jackets, black sleeveless T-shirts, custom-made zoot suits and the infamous chicken bone T-shirt which Alice Cooper bought.

While I was at the Jean Machine I had got to know Malcolm McLaren and Vivienne Westwood when I dropped into their shop. Soon after that, they shrewdly changed the name from TFTLTYTD to SEX, and the scene around the new shop became very exclusive, like a secret society. Customers didn't want to tell anyone else where they had got their clothes from, or even where the shop was, for fear of being scooped.

There were very few people in the funk scene at that time that were tapped into what Malcolm and Vivienne were doing. I definitely stood out. It was really tough breaking out of the mould dictating what black people should wear and do. There weren't many people that were brave enough to make that move, but I was one of the black people that flitted between the world of funk, reggae and this desire to be unique. Music, clothes and identity were my first steps to empowerment.

This meant that back in Brixton I was a laughing stock for a while. I was wearing wet-look peg-leg trousers with winkle-picker boots, as well as my earrings. I'd like to think people secretly admired that I had the balls to step out of the norm and go to places that other black people had not been. I was always known as the odd one out and I kind of revelled in that.

SEX was a shop with a definite ideology. It was not about selling golden oldies or any old tat, it was about creating an ATTITUDE with a capital A. The shop could be intimidating to the passer-by, or even the customers, with its blacked-out windows. Once inside there was chicken wire on the walls and excerpts from Valerie Solanis' *SCUM Manifesto* scrawled all over the place which gave the shop a dark and claustrophobic vibe.

One of the earliest SEX T-shirt designs had "You're gonna wake up one morning and know which side of the bed you've been lying on" printed on it. There were two columns, on one side were things that were "in", and on the other side things that were "out". What was cool was that it didn't specify which side was which. Listed on the T-shirt were Jamaican rude boys, Zoot suits and dreadlocks and stuff like Durrutti. It gave the notion that cultural ideas were being shared and absorbed. Bernard Rhodes designed that T-shirt. Our paths would soon cross.

In early 1975 I left Jean Machine and found myself unemployed for a while. With growing dole queues, many black families were the first to feel the heat. On the Brixton Road I stumbled across a shop called Acme which sold jukeboxes, pinball machines and one-armed bandits. The shop intrigued me and I wandered in one day and struck up a friendship with the shop's owner/manager John Krevine.

In late 1975 he decided to open a stall in the Antiquarius indoor antique market on the King's Road. As I was unemployed, had experience at Jean Machine and the gift of the gab, Krevine asked me to manage his newly named Acme Attractions stall and I accepted. On the jukebox I loaded up all my favourite reggae tunes. The Antiquarius market had some very old fogey-style antique stalls in it. There was a prehistoric atmosphere with lots of people in their fifties selling their antiques—and there was me on my stall pumping out reggae and pissing everybody off. Also in the Antiquarius market, Bernard Rhodes had a stall selling his screen-printed T-shirts and vintage reggae albums, which obviously caught my attention.

Bernard was a really interesting guy and also very politically aware. He was a player in the counter culture of the sixties. I was about sixteen years-old at the time, and Bernard made an impression on me. Later on, he would go on to manage the Clash and through my connection with them, I had a lot of dealings with him. He was always telling me to question what I did. He could always recite cultural reference points that would spark my imagination.

Between them, Bernard and Malcolm McLaren gave me a sort of alternative education, which I still draw on to this day.

8

ACME ATTRACTIONS

I first met Jeannette Lee at one of the soul nights at the Lyceum on a Monday night in early 1975. She used to go out dancing five nights a week. Before punk happened, black and white kids were mixing at places like the Bird's Nest, a chain of clubs in Waterloo, High Street Kensington and West Hampstead. The music played was James Brown, the Ohio Players, Staple Singers—mostly funk, but not Northern Soul. This is pre-dreadlocks; I had three earrings, kohl on my eyes and was wearing a see-thru plastic mac with winkle pickers.

"I thought Don was this completely unusual looking bloke in his see-thru plastic mac with loads of earrings," recalls Jeannette, "and did not look like anybody else. I was sitting on the stage and he walked straight up to me and said, 'Excuse me darling, can I sit there a minute as my shoes are killing me?'" I thought, 'How fucking rude!' But I still got up and let him sit down."

Shortly after that, I invited Jeannette to come to the Acme stall on the King's Road. She liked my plastic mac and wanted one. I wanted her to work with me at Acme. It was my way of asking her out and things went on from there. Six weeks later the stall moved to the basement and we started working together. This was Spring '75.

It was the basement version of Acme Attractions in Antiquarius that became famous. By famous, I mean as a shop/club. There was a three-piece suite in there, I had a TV, it was very personalised. It was like walking into a cool person's home. There was a clash of popular subculture all juxtaposed together that, for whatever reason, all seemed to have a common thread. Then there was me hanging around with dark glasses and dreadlocks, and Jeannette in her miniskirt and high heels.

Acme was a place to hang out, much more so than SEX was. The clothes they sold were more expensive and it could be intimidating going in the shop. In Acme you could get a pair of trousers for fifteen quid, in SEX they were fifty quid.

Our clothes were more user-friendly. Malcolm and Vivienne's shop stocked fashion as art. Acme could not claim that as far as the clothes were concerned, but as far as reflecting London's multicultural tribal mix, Acme was the place to be. If I could go back in time and do that again, I would. I was in my element.

What drew people into the basement was my soundtrack, the clothes, and Jeannette. Throughout my life, women have always been a kind of muse and inspiration to me. Jeannette and I turned each other on to new ideas, we could not get enough information. Jeannette, like a lot of white working class youth pre-punk rock, had aligned herself with black music. If it was not soul, then it was reggae.

Acme was more than just a clothes shop. It was like our private members' club, where people could meet and hang out. People would only hang out at Acme if we wanted them to. Jeannette described it as quite a hostile environment with me and my dark glasses looking intimidating. Jeannette was the user-friendly person. More people came down to see her than me or the clothes. John Beverly, before he became Sid Vicious, used to come into the shop and would be hanging on every one of Jeannette's words. He arrived once carrying a copy of *Nineteen* magazine with a picture of Bryan Ferry in it sporting a big quiff. Sid asked Jeannette, "Do you know where I could get my hair cut like that?"

In our basement the most favoured items were winkle picker shoes and peg trousers cut by a tailor that Vivienne Westwood had used. We sold the pegs that came in colours like shocking pink and electric blue. There was a scooter in the basement; the same model as the one featured in *Rebel Without a Cause*. Put it this way, if Oxford bags and platform shoes were not your thing, then you could come to Acme and check out the zoot suits, mohair three button suits and the Marlowe crêpe-soled shoes that Steve McQueen used to like. On the walls we had fifties prints of guys in Harlem wearing suits and peg trousers.

Acme was all about multiculturism, Vivienne and Malcolm's shop was more exclusive and Eurocentric—definitely not in tune with the multicultural and black aspect. They were not into that whole reggae thing that brought a lot of working class kids into Acme.

Jordan, who used to work in Malcolm and Vivienne's shop, used to hang out at Acme a lot, until Vivienne got more aggressive about people hanging out in both shops. The problem started when Acme started to make and sell the peg trousers that SEX used to sell. We also used some of the same manufacturers that SEX used for shoes. We were seen as treading on their territory. There was a guy called Vic who had a good knowledge of East End tailoring, and he had fallen out with Malcolm. He introduced us to the tailor that Malcolm and Vivienne were using.

With me being fully ensconced in the job at Acme, Vivienne now decided that I was a traitor. We had previously been good friends. There had been a brief moment while Malcolm was away in New York with the New York Dolls that she actually offered me a job, and I remember her taking me to a Lou Reed gig. We must have looked quite striking, me in my electric blue zoot suit and Vivienne in her see-thru catsuit. The main reason I had not taken up her job offer was that I could not really see myself in black patent leather gear and high heels, it would have been a move too far for me. She demanded total loyalty and commitment. You were with her or not. Having joined Acme, she banned me from her shop and never spoke to me again.

I'd go back into the shop to see my mate Michael Collins, but not when she was there. I remember being up in my bedroom trying on a rubber T-shirt he had given me. I wasn't sure I could pull off wearing it in Brixton, so I thought

I'd try it on in privacy first. I put the T-shirt on and it was very uncomfortable and hot, so I tried to take it off and it got stuck over my head. Talk about panic attack, the T-shirt was wedged around my neck and the bastard did not want to come off. It was stuck like one of those face-hugging creatures from *Alien*, and I'm suffocating, literally. So I hooked the T-shirt onto the bedpost and tried to force it off. I eventually got my breath back and the T-shirt was a heap on the floor with a huge rip in it.

At Acme my pockets were the till. There was a lot of black market culture going on in the King's Road in those days. People from different shops in the street would swap merchandise. One shop would give us smoked salmon and caviar in return for clothes. I was one of the first people to own a video—it was one of those cumbersome Philips machines. Then there was Harlequin Records—my entire record collection was thanks to Harlequin! Well, besides the reggae stuff...

When Jeannette and I started dating I was still living in the house where my brother Desmond and his family lived Brixton. In my room there was a Warhol print on the wall and a massive lava lamp; a pinball machine, one armed bandit, 8-Track music player and 'every Rasta is a star' spray painted on the ceiling. Jeannette described it as my version of a *Playboy* pad. It was not what she had expected to find in Brixton. There were records all around the room. I asked her to think of any record and I would play it. So she asked me if I had the new Jah Woosh record. It blew her mind that I had that record.

Living near me in Brixton was this old dread called Albert that we used to score weed from. Now this was a brother who had obviously smoked too much herb. He would be sitting there with his foot wired up to the light. He had a wire from his toe going to the electric socket. We asked him why, and he said, "If you're not plugged in you can't be connected." No one wanted to shake his hand. The dread was live!

Later on I moved to a grand old house in Forest Hill, built on the second highest point in London, and not long after Jeannette moved in with me. We occupied the top two floors. The other rooms were taken by JR, Leo and Tony who would later help me out at the Roxy. There was also a girl called Janice, (Jeannette's best friend), a sixteen year-old white girl. Both Joe Strummer and Chrissie Hynde also lived there at different times. Forest Hill was also the location of another near-death experience. One evening I was messing around with an air pistol and pointed it in Leo's direction, forgetting he was holding an air rifle. Leo don't play, I screamed in pain as I took one in the stomach. As revenge I later filled an ashtray with gunpowder, only it was JR that would suffer the consequences.

Janice was going through that teenage 'nobody loves me, everybody hates me, what am I gonna do with my life,' kinda years. We all got it sometimes, but Janice seemed to get it more than most.

In those days we drove around in a converted Ford Zodiac I'd bought that we called the Red Shark. The minute I started working on the King's Road, money was never a problem. I never saved for anything. If I wanted something I bought it.

The Zodiac had column gears that were converted to floor shift. It was pretty flash back then.

We'd often load up with lots of drugs and drive off to God-knows-where, returning later that night. One summer weekend everyone except for Janice decided to go for a drive to the country. She retired early to bed as me and her had just had an argument. Her constant misery brought out a nasty side in people, well me at least. When we returned that evening we noticed a funky smell, but we were so fucked we put it down to the bins or blocked drains and all crashed out. The next day Jeannette and I laid in till late as did everyone else. The reason for the lay-in, besides the obvious, was a tactic to avoid washing the dirty dishes which had piled up. Whoever rose first would have to tackle the problem out of necessity.

We decided to track down the source of the smell—we had to. After emptying the bins and checking the drains, we realised Janice's door was shut—not that odd since we assumed that she'd spent the weekend at her parents. I decided to open the door; Leo, JR and Jeannette were behind me. BAM. I'm slapped down by the smell's source. We walked into a brick wall of funk, the most sickening smell we had ever encountered. Instinctively I hit the light switch, only to see a body lying in the bed covered entirely by a sheet, where her nose was were two spots of blood. I screamed but I think the sound was only in my head and slammed the door shut. We freaked in the hallway and somehow I was nominated to go back in. Now for some strange reason I entered the room on my knees, literally crawling up to the bed and lifted the sheet to see her naked body, the upper part snow white and the part of her body that touched the bed a sickly blue. Working up all my courage I touched her body and POW she's warm. Again I reversed out of the room, fast.

There was a quick discussion about what to do. Tony remembered he'd got guests downstairs, so first thing we do is get them to leave. You know, "Excuse me but we've just found a dead body" kind of thing. Simultaneously we were freaking 'cause we were confused by the fact the body was warm. Fuck me, she could still be alive! Call the ambulance, call the police... police? Quick clear out all drugs, lose all the bent gear (bent gear was a major fringe-benefit for those operating outside the law back then). This took some time I can tell you, with numerous phone calls to friends to ferry out the contraband. When the police and ambulance arrived we all sat nervously in my room awaiting the obvious interrogation.

The police explained to us that she had apparently taken a fatal mix of Tuinal (big back then) and alcohol in a fit of depression. They knew this because she'd left a suicide note. In our mad panic we'd missed it. Furthermore because she'd left the electric blanket on she'd been slowly cooking for two days. We never found out what was in the note and for about two months everybody slept in one room—my room.

That old adage springs to mind—suicide is a permanent solution to what are often short-term problems. What a waste.

Jeannette would go on via PiL to join Rough Trade in 1987. As well as managing acts like Scritti Politti, Spiritualized and Beth Orton she now co-owns Rough Trade with Geoff Travis. She always had taste that girl.

9

SOUL SHAKEDOWN PARTY

During the mid seventies I often went to places like the Q club on Praed Street, Columbos, Upstairs at Ronnie Scott's, Trafalgar, Union Tavern and the Lacy Lady in Ilford. On the dance floor I was a flash bastard. I used to win dance competitions, and in those days you only ever ventured on to the dance floor if you had the right moves. The way you looked and your dance moves really got you the currency—and what you got with this currency was girls. Growing up within the Soul scene is where I formed the "flash git" character that would emerge at Acme Attractions. Working in clothes shops on commission taught me the psychology of how to deal with people. To get by on a day-to-day basis you have to have a dual personality; almost schizophrenic. You have to know where you are coming from and at the same time you have to compromise your personality.

The soul scene began to leave a bad taste in my mouth. It had started to develop its own prejudice. People started to look down on those who did not dress the same; the scene had become elitist and almost separatist and I was really not happy or comfortable with that. The music was good, and the political stances of a small number of the artists were commendable, but so many aspects grafted onto that scene and onto an emerging black culture in England were real BULLS-HIT!

Just listening to the music and emulating the black American blueprint was not working for me. OK, I had attended Black Panther meetings proudly wearing my Angela Davis badge, but that movement just wasn't totally relevant to the Black British experience. It didn't exactly translate to my life, which was something of a dilemma for me. I wanted to empower myself. Luckily around the same time I began to discover Rastafari through reggae.

The messages I heard through sound systems like Jah Shaka, Moa Ambassa and Coxsone were so compelling that my political and spiritual consciousness increased. This is what roots and culture does, it's literally musical reportage. Sound system was a way of imparting information; spiritually, politically, culturally. It raises awareness in all these departments, and as young black British guys, we were especially sensitive to these messages, these modes of communication.

Up until the early seventies singers like John Holt, Dennis Brown and Gregory Isaacs ruled in Jamaica, but then reggae began to change. 'Deejay' music—a rapping style created for the sound systems developed. Later on I became friendly with the three main characters; Big Youth, I-Roy and U-Roy whose music was a black aural version of CNN. Their tunes conveyed information about my culture, where I came from and what I had to offer. It seemed a whole lot more attractive and a whole lot more relevant to my situation in Britain where I was feeling alienated, downtrodden and oppressed. I was experiencing the end result of racism, being pulled up every fucking day on the streets. Reggae was more militant and seemed more identifiable to me than the Black Power struggles that were going on in America.

When I discovered Rastafari, it was not a case of just buying the records and growing the dreads, I actually went to the Ethiopian Doctrine Church and where I was coming from that was a serious commitment. But it was far too restrictive in the life journey that I had set for myself. A wise old dread once told me that there are two schools of thought—one says we are risen apes, the other that we are fallen angels—and Rastafari helped me identify with the latter. Our history predates Western history by thousands of years and it was not some mad old Rasta smoking weed that taught me that.

I was like baby dread back in those days. I was struggling with the ideals of Rastafari and how it could take me forward, whilst being confused by what I thought was some kind of a dogma. I have always had this thing where I take what I need out of something and leave the rest. The Rasta movement captured the music and minds of not only Jamaicans but also some of the 'lost tribes' in the UK of which I was part.

Listening to Bob Marley's album *Catch a Fire* was a revelation to me. Through it, I discovered the radical and politi-

cal side to reggae music. It was roots reggae which emerged
as a response to the political battles between Jamaica's two
rival political parties. The lyrical content of *Catch a Fire* was
more 'conscious' and sonically complex. Chris Blackwell had
brought in Wayne Perkins and John 'Rabbit' Bundrick to
provide the overdubs. They put some touches to the songs
that maybe Bob Marley and the Wailers would not have done,
but Bob was nobody's fool. If he had not wanted them on the
record they would not have been on it.

Tracks like "Concrete Jungle" referred to the state of
urban poverty and "Slave Driver" connected past injustices
to the present times. It was definitely more an album than a
collection of possible singles. The packaging, with the Zippo
Lighter sleeve, was also something different. Up to that time
most of the reggae sleeves looked like cheap Jamaican post-
cards. Bob Marley's 1974 album *Natty Dread* was also important to me. It too reflected on the political turmoil swallowing
up Jamaica with songs like "Three O'Clock Road Block" and
"Them Belly Full (But We Hungry)".

Dub came into its own during the early 1970s. On the B-
sides of Jamaican Rocksteady singles appeared the word 'Version'—describing an instrumental remix of the A-side that
had begun as a test for sound levels (and for somewhat obvious economic reasons was pressed on the B-side as it saved
recording another song).

Dub was the next logical step, essentially born from
a studio technique where drum and bass took centre stage.
Utilising two-track, and sometimes four-track set-ups, people
like King Tubby and Lee Perry used reverb and echo delay to

shape the sound and took the giant step of using the mixing desk as an instrument in itself. Osbourne Ruddock (aka King Tubby) was an engineer at Duke Reid's studio and began to cut dub plates of tunes with bits of the vocal left out to play on his sound system. He originally did this to offer his audience different versions of their favourite tracks. These fragments of vocals were 'flashed in' either from the A-side or a deejay would do an intro and just 'ride the riddim'. They created a sound that was then pressed onto dub plates (one-off acetates) and played by the local sound systems via valve amps and towering bass bins live and direct to the people.

Then there was Big Youth, a former cab driver in Jamaica, who served his apprenticeship with sound systems around Kingston before becoming known as the 'master deejay'. Big Youth addressed more militant things like Garveyism and Rastafari through his music. His songs were spiritual, righteous, militant and cultural. Very educational if you were black and British. The content was inspiring for a kid trying to find his feet and struggling with the duality of his existence.

Big Youth (Manley Augustus Buchanan) was one of the first to include Rasta chants with his militant deejay lyrics. He grew up in poverty in Jamaica and whilst employed as a mechanic for the Sheraton Hotel he practised his 'deejay' skills in the empty hotel rooms. His break came when he became resident DJ for the Lord Tippertone sound system. His first recording with Keith Hudson as producer, "Ace Ninety Skank", was a number one hit in Jamaica. It was his album *Screaming Target* from '73 that caught my attention. Little did I know, people like Paul Simonon and John Lydon were also listening to that album. Shortly our own two cultures would clash.

The belief of looking back to Africa to find one's identity was not just exclusive to Rastafari. In Jamaica the notion had most triumphantly been promoted by Marcus Garvey, who has often been mistaken for being Rastafari's founder. This misunderstanding was born out of the fact that Garvey has always been namechecked and praised in reggae songs. Amongst the many tributes are Burning Spear's *Marcus Garvey* album and Big Youth's track "Marcus Garvey". Born in 1887 in Jamaica, Garvey launched the Universal Negro Improvement Association in 1914 whose purpose was to give black people a government and voice of their own. Garvey strongly believed that if you were black, then you should be proud of it. Garvey was not only influential in the beginnings of Jamaican Rastafari, but he was also the spiritual father of America's black nationalists.

Religions always reflect the social and geographical environment out of which they emerge, and Jamaican Rastafari was no exception. It is very hard to define Rastafari as being a conventional religion, as all the ideas and many theories are open-ended and subject to constant evolution and individual interpretation—that is what I liked about it. Rastafari as a religion was relatively new. It was during the 1920s that Marcus Garvey said, "Look to Africa, a King will be crowned" and sure enough in the 1930s a King (Haile Selassi) was crowned. Many saw this as a fulfilment of Garvey's word—prophesy.

When Bob Marley came along, he was not just playing music, he embodied the Rasta ideology. For a young guy growing up in the middle of Babylon the message was kind of radical, and through my desperation to find out where I came from it appealed greatly. It railed against the establishment and taught me pride without having to look to the European aesthetic of beauty and values. I wanted Rastafari to empower me, not to define me. Despite the dreads and the ganja, Rastafarian ideology has much in common with the good parts of most religions. Rastafari blended the purest forms of Judaism and Christianity and accepted the Egyptian roots of both religions, whilst it did not acknowledge the Catholic Church or the Council of Rome, possibly due to the fact that Mussolini invaded Ethiopia during the thirties.

A defining Rasta belief is that combing or cutting of hair is not done. This referred to Leviticus 21:5: "They shall not make baldness upon their head, neither shall they shave off the corner of their beard". Ganja (marijuana) was regarded as "wisdom weed" and it is alleged that it was found growing on King Solomon's grave.

Things were not great between me and my parents to say the least, and the final nail in the coffin was me growing dreadlocks and starting to identify with Rastafari, something my parents' generation scorned. It was not until Bob Marley's global recognition that views softened. As far as my parents were concerned, I might as well have grown horns and a tail and been the Antichrist. Because of this, they didn't speak to me for quite a few years, apart from my dad coming to see me and saying that he wanted to sign over the land in Jamaica to me after he passed away. But there was a condition. He did not want my relatives there to see me with dreads and identifying myself with Rastafari. I told him that I could not change what I was doing as I believed in it, and to keep the land.

A lot of young people during the mid seventies were taking what they needed from Rastafari and left what they didn't— myself included. The possibility of self-interpretation was one of the attractive things about it. Rastafari's refusal to be part of daily life and commerce in "Babylon" (the establishment) appealed to the destitute and alienated and it gave them some dignity.

After a while I stopped calling myself a Rasta as I have this theory that if you label yourself, then that is all that you can be. I had already decided that I was not going to be classified by my colour or beliefs and although Rastafari was my guiding light, it was not something that I took blindly. The knowledge of Rastafari definitely took us down a better path than that of today's "Bling" culture.

Once Bob Marley came on the scene I was a changed man. He achieved status on his own terms, and not by straightening his hair or becoming Anglicised or Americanised. He was not trying to emulate things like my parents' generation who ended up being really fucked because of it. It seemed to me that if you knew where you came from, then you knew what you had to offer. The interesting dynamic of Bob was that he had the roots consciousness on one side and the rude boy rebel on the other, it was very much a double-edged sword. I went to Bob Marley's legendary gig at the Lyceum in '75 which was released as a live album. It was the closest I have ever got to a religious experience. The venue was so packed that whenever anyone moved I was lifted off the ground. It was the single most exciting music moment of my life. We were thrashing around with this British-Black, Black-British identity crisis and then the full impact and reality of what we had heard on his records all came together in that show. It was no longer an abstract thing that you could interpret one way or another. Here was the man onstage delivering it live and direct. It gave me the confidence to be myself. Bob Marley brought the politic to the forefront of reggae. It was a militant Rasta rebel vibe.

After the gig I followed Bob Marley in my car back to his hotel in Harrington Gardens, off Gloucester Road. I don't know what possessed me, I marched into the hotel with all the other Rasta brethren. Everyone was sitting down and I found a little spot in the corner. Bob was holding court in his room in the hotel and he was smoking weed and reasoning with all the Rasta elders that were coming up to him. Finally, it was three or four in the morning and Bob had out-reasoned everybody and out-smoked everybody. He looked around the room and saw me with my baby dreads and my pathetic little bag of weed. I was called to the table and reasoned with him until sunrise. After that Bob used to come into Acme Attractions to purchase a bit of weed whenever he came to London.

A few days later I went back to get a picture of Bob with myself before he returned to Jamaica. I had a Polaroid camera. All the band and Bob were like, "Bloodclaat instant picture". Polaroid technology had not yet reached Jamaica. Everybody wanted a picture of themselves and Bob. Ten pictures down, I still had not got my picture of me and Bob. Jeannette was there and she ran out to get some more film. Sure enough, another packet of Polaroids had gone and I still had not got my picture of me and Bob. Finally, with the third packet of Polaroids I got my picture.

One time we went to the Notting Hill Carnival and Bob sent me off to get some weed. He did not need weed, he was just trying to get rid of me to chat up my wife. I guess I should mention that sometime during this period I married an American girl called Marilyn—don't ask!

Bob was very much a ladies man and I loved him because of that. As well as having a dynamic side to him, he was a very real person. When I was with Bob, I was never Don Letts the film-maker. I would not have had the relationship that I had with him if I had been working or had taken advantage of the situation. I did not film him at all when he was alive.

A year or so later, when Bob Marley was staying in Oakley Street off the King's Road after he had been shot in Jamaica, I went round to his house to collect money for some weed wearing my bondage trousers. He was to all intents and purposes in exile over here and we had an argument about punk.

On seeing my bondage trousers, he exclaimed, "What ya deal wid Don Letts dem nasty punk rockers, yu look like a bloodclaat mountaineer!"

To which I replied, "Dem crazy baldheads are my mates"— or words to that effect. Needless to say, Bob became more familiar with the real deal (as opposed to the *Daily Mirror* version) during his UK stay, and was moved to record "Punky Reggae Party" a few months later.

10

DREAD MEETS
PUNK ROCKERS

"The mid-Seventies, between the first explosion of the soul boys and the new spiky heterodoxy of the punks, was the period when the parameters were pushed way back, the wardrobe was tipped up and its contents flung in all directions."

Robert Elms, *The Way We Wore*

By 1976 the writing was on the wall. John Lydon and the other guys had taken a big swipe at the pompous stadium bands with their twenty-minute solos. A typical "event" was Rick Wakeman with his *The Myths and Legends of King Arthur* extravaganza at Wembley Arena—which was as far removed from reality as you could get. My white mates were totally disillusioned with this soundtrack. ELO, ELP and Rick Wakeman's tunes said nothing about working class youth trying to survive in mid-seventies Britain. The popular music of the time no longer spoke for the people—well, none of my mates, anyway. We didn't know where California was, never mind being able to check into a goddamn hotel.

The British establishment had managed to alienate its own white youth; politically, musically, artistically and in just about every other way possible. As a first-generation British-born black of Jamaican descent, I was already well pissed off, so it was inevitable that we shared a sense of disillusionment.

A lot has been made of the interaction between the punk and reggae scenes of the late 1970s. Popular music of the previous twenty years had been informed by black music—the difference was that the punks weren't being inspired by an alien culture thousands of miles away. They were being turned on by the man next door—more River Thames than Mississippi Delta.

David Bowie and Bryan Ferry's fashion style was still making a huge impact on the King's Road. As they changed their image with each album, their fans were emulating their look, and the King's Road was the place to get the gear for Bryan Ferry's GI or Bowie's *Young Americans* look.

The different tribes were checking out Acme and SEX. There were the sixties revivalists in leather ties and Chelsea boots. There were kids in demob suits and trilbies, Bowie boys and the Americana lot in their fleck suits, the SEX bondage crowd, as well as the soul boys in their jelly sandals, see-thru macs, mohair jumpers and peg trousers.

I remember reading journalist Robert Elms' description of his first visit to Acme looking for a mohair jumper. He wrote "indeed there was a definite retro feel to Acme, with lots of Forties, Fifties and Sixties bits, old demob suits, scarlet swinging London hipsters, James Dean leather jackets, put together so that it felt terrifyingly modern, way out, confrontational and new."

The soul boys were working class white kids from the rural and suburban parts of London. They were more interested in buying hard to get hold of dance and soul imports from record shops like Contempo than getting into any band-based scene, although most of them would admit to being Bowie fans. They used to come into Acme and then go up the road to SEX to check out the competition. Some of the early punk look was built on the outside edge of that soul boy look. Those guys all used to shop at Acme, as did Chris Sullivan and his Welsh posse.

But Acme did not just outfit the soul elite, it also catered for youth whose radars were tuned into anything that was not part of the establishment or the mainstream and who were inventing their own fashion rules. We had kids from Glasgow, Huddersfield and Newcastle visiting the shop to buy Acme clothes for their nights out. Pretty quickly John Krevine decided to get stuff specially made for the shop.

The decor in the shop had evolved even more, and was very distinctive—plastic palm trees, posters of the Beatles and reggae artists and, of course, the Mod scooter remained parked in the middle of the floor. We decorated one wall with pink and blue teardrop-shaped sunglasses.

The jukebox played an eclectic mix of reggae and early New York punk. The stock was constantly changing; we sold clothing that was original, but also elegant with a nod to the Fifties and Sixties. There was this guy called Jack English, an original Mod, that used to bring in Wemblex pin-collar shirts and sunglasses. Although we sold clothes from the Forties, Fifties and Sixties, I never considered Acme to be retro. It was stuff that most people had never seen before, so therefore it looked futuristic.

At that time the King's Road was full of drugs—and if you wanted to get some weed you could come to Acme. I can remember doing acid at Acme Attractions a couple of times. Not the best idea, being in a basement. I am talking about real acid. You could see the carpet melting, you could see the devil sitting next to you. I recall Antonio, a South American gay hairdresser that Jeannette married so that he could stay in the country—he got killed by a lorry soon after—brought in someone that I thought looked familiar to buy some weed. As we're doing the deal I eased down my shades (worn constantly since about '75) and realised I was face-to-face with Peter O'Toole. He lowered his regular glasses, put his finger to his lips and left.

As I was behind the counter every day at Acme with Tappa Zukie's *MPLA Dub* booming out of the speakers, burning spliffs and holding my corner, I started to notice the same white faces coming down to the basement. These guys were checking me out and I was checking them out. It was like some kind of macho stand off, like in a Peckinpah Western.

The guys were John Lydon, Paul Simonon and Joe Strummer. Initially we said nothing to each other and just observed. It was Jeannette that got to know them at first, and I was pretty pissed off as I did not want anyone to steal my thunder—or my girlfriend. Maybe, if it had not been for Jeannette, I would have stayed like that.

Eventually everyone dropped their guard and we started talking about reggae and dub music whilst sharing a spliff in the basement. I quickly became friendly with Strummer and Simonon, but John Lydon caught my imagination in particular. John had an aura that attracted people to him, which I believe stemmed from the fact that he was very self-aware. Joe Strummer was smart too. Joe and John were the brains behind what was emerging. These guys were already into reggae and were seriously interested in the stuff I was pumping out.

They were familiar with tracks like "Liquidator" and "The Return of Django". Paul Simonon had grown up in Brixton and Notting Hill and was well-informed about Jamaican culture and the music. I was coming in with King Tubby and Lee Perry's heavy dub. I was also playing things like Keith Hudson's *Pick A Dub*, a set of records called *African Dub Chapters 1,2* and *3*, the Big Youth album *Dreadlocks Dread* and Tappa Zukie's *Man Ah Warrior* album. *King Tubby meets the Rockers Uptown* with Augustus Pablo was my theme tune. Lydon and the Clash guys liked the music that I was playing in the shop and we realised that we had a shared interest. They dug the bass lines and the fact that the music was saying something. They didn't mind the weed either.

Because of the position I was in at Acme, we gravitated towards each other. I can remember later hanging out with John Lydon after the Pistols' gig at the Nashville. We went back to my house in Forest Hill and spent the whole night talking about reggae music and Jamaican culture. We also used to hang out at the Roebuck in Chelsea which became the punk rock pub, so to speak. I used to spend my time in the pub having many intellectual arguments with John Bindon (R.I.P) who had been in *Performance* and Ken Loach's *Poor Cow* film in the sixties, a grim portrayal of life on the breadline, shot in a documentary style. John Bindon was well-known in the sixties and seventies as an actor who played violent characters on screen, and in real life he was a gangster with royal connections, not someone you'd want to mess with. He was also an associate of the Krays and the Richardsons. I spent many afternoons in the Roebuck discussing and debating with him. He admired the fact that I could hold my own.

Both John Lydon and Sid Vicious came to Acme to get clothes as they found it cheaper than SEX up the road. One time at Acme we sold Keith Moon's jacket to Sid and told him it used to be Elvis Presley's. The people who sold it to us told us it had belonged to Elvis, but in reality Keith Moon had worn it in the film *Stardust*. I wore it for a while and then Sid bought it; then John wore it and Viv Albertine from the Slits wore it for a long time.

Sid to me was just plain old John Beverley. He wasn't the monster that the press made him out to be—yet. I remember him as being shy and quiet, gullible even. He believed his own press which was just very sad. He took a definite shine to Jeannette, but then again, everyone did.

We used to go to a restaurant called Up All Night on the Fulham Road after we'd been to the Roxy. Sid used to tag along with us. We'd be eating our food and he would be annoying the other customers by burping in their faces or trying to fart on them. Once I was on the tube with him and he gobbed on the windows and licked it off. You should have seen the passengers' faces. Sid used to do things that would draw attention to him. It was sad to see him take on the Vicious persona. Quite often when he got into fights with people, he would come off worse.

I recently watched Alex Cox's *Sid and Nancy*. I saw it the first time round and I did not warm to it, as it was too soon after Sid's death. I saw it the other day and I had to keep reminding myself no, that's not Sid that's Gary Oldman. What an incredible actor.

Chrissie Hynde was one of a trio that used to come down to Acme with Judy Nylon and Patti Palladin. Judy and Patti went on to form a band called Snatch and Patti did a lot of work with Johnny Thunders and the Heartbreakers. Chrissie used to hang out at Acme regularly and quickly made an impression on me, as she knew all about the American people like Richard Hell and Patti Smith, whilst I reciprocated by turning her onto reggae. She was not living anywhere permanently and was working as a cleaner to make money. I gave her cash so that she could eat and she did some T-shirts for us which we used to sell. At that time she had just arrived back from Paris after living with the journalist Nick Kent and was writing for the *NME*. Eventually Chrissie came to live in Forest Hill with myself and the other Rasta brethren, and later on Joe Strummer lived there as well for a short while. She wanted me to join her band, but I had to explain to her that I could not play an instrument. Chrissie and I have remained close friends and it was her that encouraged me to stop eating meat.

I was the man when it came to compilation tapes. In those days they were cultural currency. People like Lenny Kaye and Patti Smith, John Lydon, the Clash and the Slits would take them out on the road with them. Patti walked in one day with Lenny. They had found out I knew Tappa Zukie and were crazy about his album *Man Ah Warrior*. Patti expressed an interest in meeting Tappa and invited us all to her sold out gig at the Hammersmith Odeon. So we're standing in the wings watching the show when Patti pulls me on stage and hands me her guitar. We're live in front of 3,000 people. I had never been on stage in my life and could not play guitar—worries! I decided to front it out and pretended to play. Dark glasses hid my terror. Tappa and Jeannette are laughing their heads off in the wing, so I grab Tappa and pull him onstage swiftly handing him the guitar! Breathing a sigh of relief I try and exit stage left, just as Patti decides to hand me her mic, BLOOD-CLAAT!!!

She grabs another guitar and lies down on the floor at my feet. I break into my heaviest Jamaican accent so that no one could hear that I didn't know what I was babbling about. Needless to say there was 'nuff "cramp and paralyse them and those who worship Babylon" type stuff to cover the bluff. I look to my right, Tappa is rocking pretending to play guitar, I look to my feet, Patti is writhing on the floor, I look at the audience and they're buying it. Jah Rastafari!

11

NO DON'T STOP THE CARNIVAL

"London is the place for me."
                                        Lord Kitchener

"Things ain't what they used to be."
                                        Tommy Steele

London's first Caribbean Carnival was held in St Pancras
Town Hall in January 1959. The idea stemmed from a meeting at the Brixton office of the *West Indian Gazette* a few
months earlier. Claudia Jones, who worked for the paper,
wanted to do something to improve the morale of the West
Indian Community in Notting Hill. Race Riots had spread
from Nottingham to Notting Hill during 1958 when locals
waged their racial war on the newly settled West Indian community.

The black community had had enough of racism and racist
abuse and attacks. Someone at the *Gazette* came up with the
idea of having a Carnival. Held at the Town Hall, the Carnival went well, with dancing, lots of curried goat, rice and peas.

That evening saw the beginnings of the black community getting back to its cultural roots and de-Anglicising itself.

From then on Carnival was held each year alternating between the Seymour Hall and the Lyceum. It was not until 1965 that it was held in Notting Hill after Rhaune Laslett, a Notting Hill resident, spoke to the police about holding a carnival there. She wanted to involve all of the community; Irish, Spanish, Caribbeans, Africans and Portuguese to name a few. Notting Hill at that time was a piss-poor area, but it had a real multicultural vibe to it. Laslett ran the Carnival for several years and the attendance grew to about 10,000 people. The event was a great success and blurred the lines between participant and spectator and quickly became a symbol of freedom.

By 1976 Carnival had become a predominantly Caribbean event built on Jones' racial offensive and Laslett's cooperative activism. For my parents' generation the Carnival was a show of pride in the face of prejudice. The riot that year kicked off after police tried to arrest a pickpocket close to Portobello Road. Several black youths went to help the guy and it escalated into a riot. The police grabbed dustbin lids to protect themselves from the bricks and debris raining down on them. At one point a police van was set alight and the coppers only just managed to get out before it was engulfed in flames. Over one hundred police officers had to be taken to hospital after the riot. Many were released after treatment, but at least twenty were kept in for observation or further treatment. Sixty carnival-goers were also taken to hospital and at least sixty people were arrested.

To this day people think that there was a racial theme to the riot in 1976, but to my mind it was not a black or white thing. It was a wrong or right thing. Working class people being harassed by the police. Hence the Clash song "White Riot", with the words "Black man gotta lotta problems/but they don't mind throwing a brick." The Clash were saying, "look our black brethren have had enough and they have done something about it." The song was misunderstood by some as being a right-wing song.

During the Notting Hill riot I was wandering around with my Super-8 camera, torn between getting the shot and throwing a brick. The infamous picture of me that ended up on the front of the *Blackmarket Clash* album was taken at this time. It looks like I am fronting the cops off, but I am actually crossing the road. Behind me are 500 brothers all armed with bottles and bricks and the police lines were right in front of me. It was best that I moved out of the way. Joe Strummer and Paul Simonon were also caught up in it. They were throwing bricks. The white youth were right in there alongside the black youth, including myself, all sick to death of the SUS law.

The SUS law was a stop-and-search policy based upon Sections 4 and 6 of the Vagrancy Act, 1824, which made it illegal for a suspected person to loiter in a public place. It gave the police the power to stop and search anyone that they had even a slight suspicion about. SUS was routinely abused, usually to the detriment of black youth who were regularly harassed for doing no more than just being on the street and being black. For some reason during the mid-seventies I seemed to be the ultimate victim of the SUS law, pretty much every week I was stopped by the Old Bill.

In those days I still had the flashy Zodiac car. I used to drive around with John Lydon and Jeannette and whenever we saw a group of Teds I used to drive past them real slow. It used to really freak them out seeing John Lydon in the car driven by dreadlocked man with dark glasses, leopard-skin waistcoat and a leather jacket with natty dread on the back of it. It was a total culture clash, and they'd be thinking, "What the fuck is going on here?" If I had been a cop, I would have pulled me up. One time I was told that, "People with red, gold and green hats shouldn't have enough money to drive flash cars." Eventually I got an old battered Morris Minor and was never pulled up again.

If you were unlucky you were pulled up by the Old Bill, but if you were pulled up by the SPG then you were fucked. The Special Patrol Group used to implement the SUS laws, mainly on black youth, and that usually meant a good kicking in the back of one of their vans. I have not met a black man yet that was not stopped as a teenager growing up in seventies Britain. It is said that one out of thirty-five people that were stopped were arrested.

It was fucking ridiculous. If I went to the cinema I had to schedule an extra half hour, because I knew that I would probably get pulled up and miss the start of the film. When I saw a police car behind me, I pulled over before they could pull me over. I used to walk up to the cops and say, "Look, what do you want? You make me really nervous when you are behind me, you are going to make me crash, let's get it over with." I was not a criminal. It got to a point where I got kind of bolshie about it. I remember one particular time they pulled me up somewhere off the King's Road, Chelsea. I got out of the car and jumped up onto the bonnet and I was like, "Yo, what are you guys trying to do, crucify me?" and all of a sudden passers-by were watching me.

If you were pulled up in the middle of the night however, with no witnesses you really were screwed. All of a sudden you'd fall over and break your arm getting into the police van. From that point on, every time I got pulled up on the street I would stand with my legs spread-eagled and my arms in the air, sort of American stylee.

The cops would be shocked and say, "Look young man, there is no need for that."

I would reply, "It is OK officer, I feel a lot more comfortable like this, and then you cannot say I have done anything wrong."

The minute you did that on the street everybody was looking. I flipped the script on them. I even remember being pulled up in various places and I used to start taking my clothes off and walking around in my fucking underpants and they were totally shocked. It was taking control of the situation.

Having said that, there were times when I was busted by the cops and rightly so. One day as I was walking down the King's Road with my mate Antonio smoking a spliff, I remember sensing something was wrong. I turned around and there was a plain clothes cop behind us. I legged it and Antonio got caught. I went back and said, "It was my first spliff and it was my first puff." We got let off with a bollocking.

After that the Chelsea police got familiar with me, and over the next few years working on the King's Road, I got busted another three times. On one particular occasion I was driving up to Acme with Jeannette and I had a load of weed on me. We were busted by the police and they let Jeannette go. As Jeannette was a beautiful white girl, about five foot nothing tall, they let her walk. But they decided to bust me and my pet ferret.

Oh yeah, I forgot to mention that at that time I had a ferret. Bryan Ferret—don't ask!

So they busted me and the ferret, and took us to Chelsea nick. As I say, I got quite familiar with the Chelsea Old Bill and every time they passed the shop they would say, "Alright Don?"

One night I went to the Scala with some of my Rasta brethren from the Roxy to see a Clint Eastwood triple bill. We sat there watching the first movie, smoking spliffs. During the second movie we were still smoking spliffs. Before the third movie started there was a break. So we went to the canteen area, and all of a sudden about fifteen Old Bill came in and busted me. Before I had seen the bloody last film! It transpired that some off-duty cops had been sat behind us for the whole of the first two movies and must have called their mates. You have to wonder if the Old Bill were sitting there watching the movies, relating to Clint—I know we were, but in reality we were miles apart.

Nowadays the Notting Hill Carnival has grown to be the biggest 'street' festival in Europe. Over a million pleasure-seekers every year cause a roadblock in the heart of London, oblivious to the Carnival's political, social and historical background. From its early days, it was controlled by the first Trinidadian settlers of Ladbroke Grove, but it was not long before all the Islands found a voice at Carnival. It was nearly hi-jacked by the Jamaican sound systems in the seventies and that's where I came in, listening to sounds with names like 'Shaka' and 'Coxsone Sound'. After an initial sound clash, a balance was struck. Reggae and Calypso provided a running commentary on current events. Journalism set to music. And if you can resist the smell of the various foods on sale then you are a slimmer man than I.

Today regular fixtures like Norman Jay's 'Good Times Sound-System' and Gaz's 'Rockin Blues' really capture the evolution of the carnival sound. One of my favourite spots is on the junction of All Saints Road and Westbourne Park Road; sound systems piled stories high on every corner, just as the steel band pulls in. Calypso, Soca, Soul, Ragga, Reggae and Hip-Hop. The tree-lined harmony of west London gets slapped upside the head. Ladbroke Grove—Ladbroke groove—dubtown.

Dressing up in costume is also an integral part of the Carnival. On the night before the 1991 Carnival, I went on a 'recce' to the headquarters of 'Perpetual Beauty', one of the hundreds of Mas Bands who parade over the two days. It was two in the morning and an operation of military proportions was in progress. Young and old were busy putting the final touches to the fantastic costumes that are so much a part of the Carnival. After a year of unseen preparation, their creations, like butterflies live for a brief moment and the very next day work begins on next year's creations.

I've grown up with Carnival. I remember burning in the 'Metro', reasoning with Bob Marley, the treble and the bass beneath the Westway and the warrior charge of Aswad live until midnight...

Carnival is not a spectator sport, it is like life, if you stand and stare, it'll just pass you by...

12

ONE HUNDRED DAYS

The Roxy Club was started by Andrew Czezowski (along with Sue Carrington and Barry Jones) as a direct response to an emerging scene that already had a new soundtrack and a new attitude, but no place to play. Andrew was aware of the buzz created by the music I was playing in the shop, so he asked me to DJ there on a regular basis, and I hesitantly took the job. It meant I was perfectly placed to witness the most exciting and inspiring period of my life.

There were no UK punk records to play as none had been made yet. So in between the fast and furious punk sets I played some serious dub reggae, although I did spin some MC5, Stooges, Ramones and New York Dolls. Most of the upcoming punk bands owned the first two Dolls' albums and many actually learned to play by listening to the Ramones' debut album. Speed was usually the drug of choice whilst listening to the Detroit garage bands, but once that heavy bass dropped on a Prince Far I track like "Under Heavy Manners", spliffs were definitely the order of the day. There was only one deck working at the Roxy, and I never played requests. Why hear something you have heard before when you can hear something new?

The *Dread Meets Punk Rockers Uptown* compilation I put together recently was an example of those nights. It is a selection of what I played in the Roxy and in the basement of Acme Attractions; an easy task as reggae was going through a really creative phase during the mid- to late-Seventies. Amongst the tracks are King Tubby's "Bag A Wire Dub", "Fisherman" by the Congos and the mighty "MPLA Dub" by Tappa Zukie.

The Roxy opened in what had been an old gay club called Chagaramas in Covent Garden, which was then a few run-down vegetable warehouses, as the fruit and veg market had moved to Nine Elms. The Roxy had a small upstairs reception room with a bar, and downstairs was a stage and dance-floor surrounded by bench seats and mirrored walls. It completed the third essential ingredient of any serious musical movement; the bands, a set of characters and an HQ or a base where these elements could feed off each other. Up until that point, the only place where these like-minded outlaws could meet in London was a gay club called Louise's, but the punk rockers were only guests and there were no live bands.

I went back to Forest Hill and told my brethren that I had got the gig DJ'ing at the Roxy. They could not stop laughing and taking the piss. Andrew was looking for staff, so I asked them if they were interested and they said, "Get the fuck out of here." I got them to come down to the Roxy, and they saw an untapped herb market before their eyes, so a week later all my Rasta mates from Forest Hill were working there. The punks could not roll their own spliffs, so the guys swiftly decided to sell ready-rolled ones behind the bar. I can remember Shane McGowan coming up and saying, "Give me a spliff and two beers please," and after a moment's hesitation, "No make that two spliffs and one beer!" There was some serious cultural exchange going on in the Roxy.

I played my Dub reggae sounds in between sets by the Clash, the Damned, the Buzzcocks, the Slits, Generation X, the Banshees and many more. The Sex Pistols never played the Roxy. Malcolm McLaren didn't want to give approval to something he couldn't control. Upstairs the toilets were rammed with kids jacking speed, downstairs the Rasta bredrin were selling weed and for a brief moment in time there was a punky reggae party. We had kids queuing up to get tickets in their school uniforms. Jimmy Page of Led Zeppelin came down to check the Damned one time. My brother Desmond, who was the doorman, took a perverse pleasure in 'fucking with him'.

Inspired by the punk DIY ethic (and seeing the Pistols), punk bands started springing up all over the UK and the Roxy was where many got their first break. All the hardcore dub stuff I was playing was the antithesis of the punk stuff, which was speedy. I came to realise that it was really a welcome break having these dub interludes between the punk bands. It has to be said that 70% of them were shit, real rubbish in amongst true moments of genius.

Of course this was around the time that the 'pogo' phenomenon erupted on the dance floor (courtesy of Sid Vicious) along with that other strange punk habit: 'gobbing'—basically the audience spitting at the bands while they performed. I have to stress that during 'our' period at the Roxy, nobody gobbed at anybody. Partially because the scene hadn't deteriorated into the post-Grundy tabloid-punk circus it became, but mostly because of Big Joe (one of my Rasta bredrin), who was effectively a bouncer who stood in front of the stage while the bands performed.

This period firmly established the Roxy as the home of punk rock in the UK and it quickly became a magnet to the New York crowd as the notoriety spread like wildfire. In America nobody took any notice of punk rock, so people like Jayne County—then known as Wayne County—and Johnny Thunders came to England, and via the Roxy they got their second chance. Johnny Thunders and the Heartbreakers rocked like motherfuckers. The thing that stopped them in their tracks (no pun intended) was heroin. The Heartbreakers and Nancy Spungen single-handedly brought heroin into the UK scene, before that it was ganja and speed. With Nancy and Johnny smack became fashionable and that was the end of one stage of punk rock and an indicator that things were changing. I always had a lot of time for Wayne County, who had one hell of a legacy, starting well before the New York Dolls. He was in Warhol's *Pork*.

The Clash played at the Roxy on January 1st 1977. I could not understand a fucking word they were singing, but the energy was like being hit over the head with a plank. You could not just be a fan, you wanted to be part of it, you wanted to get involved. Watching the Clash or the Pistols on stage was like somebody dropping a match into a box of fireworks. I already had Bob Marley, dub and roots reggae, and added the Clash and the Sex Pistols—it was like having thunder in one hand and lightning in the other. Even though I had my own anti-establishment thing going with reggae, seeing the Pistols and the Clash live for the first time was year zero. I also saw the Pistols at Brunel University, the Nashville and at the Screen on the Green, which I filmed and formed part of what would later become *The Punk Rock Movie*. I only got a few numbers down, as Malcolm McLaren saw me filming and threw me out. You bastard Malcolm!

About this time I was interviewed about my Beatles' memorabilia collection. During the interview I was thinking "this is complete bullshit" and I stopped the interview. The next day I swapped my entire collection for a car. It was a metallic blue version of the *Starsky and Hutch* car, massive back wheels and everything. The Old Bill made it impossible for me to hang on to that. I got rid of a lot of great music that I was listening to because of the year zero of punk rock. There were albums by Bob Dylan, Led Zeppelin and Pink Floyd. I wiped the slate clean when punk came along. We all got rid of our record collections, but what was more interesting was that we had them in the first place. In subsequent years, we all ended up buying those records back. All counter culture becomes appropriated until the next movement comes along to react against it. It becomes this thing that the next lot have to rebel against; you almost need it to happen. Sometimes you have to get ill before you find the medicine to get better.

Myself, John Lydon, Joe Strummer and Arianna from the Slits used to spend many smoky nights wedged up against the bass bins in the Four Aces reggae club in Dalston. It was a dark and tiny room with speakers up to the ceiling. Every second someone used to drop from a combination of the weed, the drink, the heat and the bass. It was the heaviest reggae club in the country and Lydon, Strummer and Arianna were the only white faces to be seen. They got a lot of respect, mainly because they had the balls to walk in the club in the first place. Arianna and I went to many reggae clubs in those days. There were sound clashes like Coxsone vs Saxon that used to happen at the local Town Halls.

If I was going to a reggae show and John or Joe was around, I would invite them along. One time I took Joe to the Hammersmith Palais, a night that would inspire him to write "White Man in Hammersmith Palais". He had gone down there to see this Roots Rockers Ghetto kind of show, not realising that the brothers back home were not revelling in a ghetto lifestyle. The ghetto is something that you get out of, not into, and Joe had a romanticised idea of what ghetto life was about. So what Joe describes in the song was getting something quite glam and glitzy and being taken by that.

Sound system traditionally had a way of delivering information that was spiritual, cultural and political. As a young black British guy, I was sensitive to the messages in the songs: "Burn Down Babylon", "I Need a Roof Over My Head", "Money In My Pocket", "Police and Thieves" and

"Two Sevens Clash. The punks were very receptive too. The Clash had slogans painted on their clothes like "Hate and War" and "Under Heavy Manners" that were influenced by phrases from Tappa Zukie, Prince Far I and Culture's music. The Clash and Johnny Rotten understood and aligned themselves with reggae's revolutionary stance and ruthless hate of the establishment. For the punks it was a choice. We were black and had no choice.

All this energy came out in such a short space of time. During the days I'd be working at Acme, before leaving for my evening stint at the Roxy. In between spinning my tunes I'd watch the bands I liked, or laugh at the ones I didn't. The original Roxy only lasted for 100 days, it was like going on tour without moving with all the acts that I saw play there. I have vivid memories of dropping acid (again) when I had a cyst on my eye. It burst while I was in the DJ booth, so I had to go to the hospital tripping out of my bonce and after getting medical treatment I came back and carried on DJ'ing. On another night the Roxy was actually robbed by a bunch of phoney villains posing as coppers. They locked Andy in a cupboard and went off into the night with the evening's takings

At the end of March 1977 the landlords ousted Andy and his crew. My brethren and me 'walked' as a show of solidarity.

13

DREAD WITH A CAMERA

What I picked up most from mixing with the punks was a new way of approaching things—that whole punk DIY ethic. In third world countries, the DIY ethic is second nature, it is DIY or die. Punk gave me the ammunition to formularise that DIY ethic artistically. The seventies film and music scene had been based on that old-boy network and there was a lot of mystique around it. Punk stripped a lot of that away. The DIY ethos was a blueprint for the working class to create their own shit despite the class system and the closed doors of the old-boy network.

Punk was magnetic. I felt an affiliation. The whole era made people realise the creative potential within themselves. The shit I learned then still works for me today. Apart from hip-hop, no other movement since punk has had content and weight going way beyond the music. Punk, like hip-hop, came from people who had nothing and used what they had to get what they wanted. I came to realise that a good idea attempted was better than a bad idea perfected. So with the birth of Punk Rock I literally reinvented myself as "Don Letts the film-maker". It has been said that when people saw the Pistols or the Clash play, half of them formed a band the next day, which is partially true. But many people, myself included, left those gigs and took the inspiration and the attitude and it informed whatever we did, or were going to do. Instead of hero-worshipping those groups, I thought, "Hey, I can do something too." That was the message. It was about using what you had to get what you wanted. Inspired by this ethic, everyone was picking up guitars and the stage soon became full. I wanted something different. I picked up a Super-8 camera.

Caroline Baker, a fashion stylist at the time (*Nova*, *The Sunday Times*) used to come into Acme to see what was going on at the grass roots level of things. We became friends and she bought me a Super-8mm camera. She saw that I wanted to do something and was in a position to help me out. There was a lot of that going on within the punk rock movement. Instead of getting through the door and slamming it shut, you got through the door and left it open to let other people through.

I had seen *The Harder They Come* and it had a big affect on me. I was also taken with the underground, DIY feel to John Waters' film *Female Trouble*. While I was at Acme, John Krevine turned me on to John Waters. I had never seen *Pink Flamingos* and *Female Trouble* and what captured my imagination was that those films had gained a cult status without anybody being able to see them.

Around this time I also discovered a Melvin Van Peebles film called *Sweet Sweetback Badaasssss Song*. In a similar way to the John Waters films, *Badaasssss* built a reputation so quickly, that once word got around, if you had not seen it you really had to check it out.

Sweet Sweetback Badaasssss Song was the first blaxploitation film and the highest grossing independent film of 1971. It told the story of Sweetback, played by Melvin himself. Sweetback ends up a fugitive in LA after retaliating when the cops beat up a political activist. Whilst on the run, Sweetback takes some time out for some love making and to beat a few people up himself. One thing that really impressed me was the line in the credits: "Starring the Black Community". The unions would have immediately put an abrupt stop to Melvin's film-making if they had known that he had a multiracial crew working for him, but he convinced them that he was making a porn movie and got away with it.

It is an angry film, and has such a high level of energy that even the Black Panthers were down with it. It is said that *Shaft* was originally going to be a white movie with a white lead actor, but when *Sweet Sweetback Badaasssss Song* came along, *Shaft* became a black movie with a black lead actor. *Sweetback* made being revolutionary and politically informed attractive and important. Without this movie there probably would not have been *Black Caesar*, *Cleopatra Jones* and *Truck Turner* amongst others. Quentin Tarantino and Spike Lee both took considerable notice of those early blaxploitation films.

But it was *The Harder They Come* that gave me a true feeling of empowerment. It gave blacks in Britain a sense of identity that was much more relevant than *Shaft* or *Superfly*. *The Harder They Come* taught me a lot about my culture, much of which I had been unaware of up until that point. I had already grasped the musical element of life in Jamaica, it was this film that gave me the visual element.

The Harder They Come was the first film project that Island Records' Chris Blackwell became involved with, and Perry Henzell did a good job of directing a brutally honest depiction of ghetto life in Jamaica with no attempt to romanticise it. Jimmy Cliff, the star of the film, was not a trained actor, so that also added an element of realism.

Cliff plays a character called Ivan, who comes to Kingston looking for work. He finds it impossible to get a job, so he decides to make music. He quickly realises that the recording industry is just as corrupt as the world outside of it and finds himself becoming a Jesse James-type hero. The film was loosely based on the story of a forties gangster called Rhygin, who killed three policemen before being shot attempting to escape to Cuba by boat.

When Ivan first comes to Kingston he goes to the cinema and gets caught up in the on-screen drama; but the local wide-boy, Jose, tells him that the hero cannot die until the last reel. Ivan goes and lives the movie for real and dies in a shoot out in the last reel. It is a great scene that parallels the whole movie. When Jose is run out of town by Ivan, all through the altercation between them "Pressure Drop" by the Maytals is simmering underneath. The way Henzell interweaves the music within the storyline is remarkable. What other movie single-handedly broke a music genre all across the planet?

The marriage of the soundtrack and narrative in *The Harder They Come* left an impression on me that has inspired my life and work.

Perry Henzell shot the film in places we had never seen before—in the ghetto, in the gutter, not the postcard Jamaica. Henzell was influenced by the French New Wave films, using flash frames and cross cutting. In the final scene, he cut out every fourth frame, which had a devastating effect.

If I manage to make a film as good as *The Harder They Come* in my lifetime, I will die a happy man.

When Chris Blackwell first met Bob Marley, he thought Bob was the "living embodiment" of the rebel outlaw and street poet portrayed by Jimmy Cliff's character in the film. For me, it was telling how closely I could relate to *The Harder They Come*, even though it was far removed from my experience as a black youth in the UK. I liked the idea that *The Harder They Come* raised awareness of Jamaican culture and entertained at the same time. It must have had the same impact on me as *Rebel Without a Cause* must have had on young white kids in the fifties.

I can specifically remember seeing Cocteau's *Orphée*. It was like poetry on celluloid, and for its time Cocteau's cinematic tricks were no mean feat. During the film there is some really weird stuff going on, like coded messages being sent via a radio. Another film that impressed me was *The Battle of Algiers*, the story of a conman who joins Algerian guerrillas to fight against the French government. The particularly intriguing thing is that it is really hard to tell if it is a documentary or a film. I have not seen anything to this day that matches it. I was also impressed by *El Topo*—a mythological spin on the life of Jesus. A truly amazing film.

Mean Streets and *Taxi Driver* have also been a huge inspiration to me. Those films represented a new visual language. *Mean Streets* provided the blueprint for *The Sopranos* and the film proved that Scorsese was a genius at integrating music and image. It has been said that the film was shot on a handheld camera for flexibility and to save time. Scorsese initially showed the film to John Cassavetes who told him, "Don't cut it, whatever you do!" and I am glad he didn't.

Before *Mean Streets* I had admired the films of Michael Powell and Emeric Pressburger, who also influenced and inspired Martin Scorsese. They made films that had an element of fantasy to them but were misunderstood at the time by film critics and audiences alike. Winston Churchill even tried to ban their film *The Life and Death of Colonel Blimp*. What I liked about their films was that the traditional storytelling was executed in such a beautiful way (for example *The Red Shoes* and *Black Narcissus*). The tracking, the camera moves, and the way that it segues from one scene to the next is truly amazing. For the most part it was crafted storytelling. The technical aspects of their films were so intricate, unless you are tuned into that stuff it is hard to notice.

The abrupt end of Powell's career can be pinned down to one film, *Peeping Tom*. An uncompromising portrait of madness, it is the story of a young man who murders women, using a movie camera to film their dying expressions of terror. Powell cleverly makes a sober study of sexual violence, as well as a meditation on voyeurism. He creates a garish red and pale blue twilight landscape of backstreet London in perfect detail. The film opened to scathing reviews in April 1960. Years later, Scorsese heralded the film as an English classic that said all there is to say about directing.

They say the true sign of genius is inconsistency and this could well apply to another of my favourite directors—Nick Roeg. His trademarks were the use of colour, combined with intercutting scenes, a willingness to be experimental and an attention to detail. Watching *Walkabout* helped me become visually aware of the delivery of the story. Roeg did not follow that A to B to C route—the film did not run from beginning to middle to end, there were all these weird tangents. For example, in *Walkabout* there is the city and wilderness, wilderness and city, death and life, life and death. Roeg's films have a sense of adventure and also deal with moral issues. For him, location has always been important. In *Walkabout* he showed an appreciation of the mysterious Australian outback and also a sense of fear of the undiscovered. He touched on the same theme with the canals of Venice in *Don't Look Now*, starring Donald Sutherland and Julie Christie as a husband and wife coming to terms with the recent loss of their daughter in a drowning accident. The film was mostly shot on location there and I would consider it to be his most compassionate and fatalistic work.

Roeg was again to explore the theme of alienation in *Performance*. A visually compelling and disturbing look at two diverse sides of 1960s London; the criminal underworld and hippie culture. Robert Fox plays a gangster fugitive who takes refuge in the Notting Hill home of Turner (played by Mick

Jagger) a semi-retired bisexual rock musician. Turner becomes infatuated with Chas' violent charisma and his "vital energy" he himself feels he has lost. As the title suggests, the film is all about performances and role reversal. Full of Roeg's visual flourishes it's still my favourite London movie and features one of the best soundtracks ever.

Roeg continued challenging the industry with *The Man Who Fell to Earth*, with the inspired choice of David Bowie playing an alien visiting earth, telling a tale of how the American dream had been hijacked by consumerism, and had a deeper message than your usual sci-fi rubbish. I also really enjoyed *Eureka* which dealt with one's wildest dreams coming true in mid-life.

It was Orson Welles who said, "If you want to make an original film—don't watch films." I learned the technical aspects of film-making from seeing the beauty of Powell and Pressburger's work or watching the Ealing films like *Passport to Pimlico*. But it was through *The Harder They Come* and punk rock that I got the vibe that I wanted to express myself visually.

14

TYPICAL GIRLS

In Spring 1977, John Krevine and Steph Raynor decided to close Acme Attractions and leave the basement that had become a hive of cultural exchange. They started a shop called Boy, which was located halfway between Sloane Square and World's End on the King's Road. Boy sold T-shirts with mock-up death images of Gary Gilmore on them and jewellery made from hypodermic syringes. On the walls were framed newspaper pages with the headline 'Boy' on each page. Krevine told the *Evening News* that the clothes were about "survival in London in 1977".

Raynor and Krevine started copying the punk rock uniform, and I for one was not comfortable with that. After the Grundy TV interview with the Pistols, the whole country thought they knew about punk and it heralded the start of the tabloid punk movement. From the "Filth and the Fury" headlines in the *Daily Mirror*, people were being told how to dress like a punk. It was amazing how ugly people could make themselves look even uglier. The secondhand punks looked fucking ridiculous. The inner circle was very stylish. Nobody we knew had staples in their noses or mothball earrings.

I ran Boy with Jeannette, but I can honestly say that I could not hold my head up when I was running that joint. When the shop first opened they decided to generate some controversy and put in a window display that had forensic sculptures of a burnt foot and hand made by artist Peter Christopherson. It was supposed to shock and cause a storm. Two nurses swore blind that the body parts were real and called the police. I was taken to court and charged under some Napoleonic law stating that soldiers coming back from war were not allowed to exhibit their war wounds for financial gain. I was prosecuted for indecent exhibition—which made me sound like a flasher. I have always resented the fact that I was charged for it. If I was driving a bus and there was an ad on the bus that was offensive, would they charge the bus driver?

As Boy opened, punk had reached its peak—there were even tabloid-fuelled Teddy Boy versus Punk battles on the King's Road. We were right in the middle of the bloody King's Road and the fights would be happening from Sloane Square, past Boy, all the way up to World's End where Vivienne and Malcolm's shop was. The Teds, who were sort of old-school, were forty and fifty year-old geezers who arrived with their ten year-old kids dressed up in drape jackets. Many a time I saw a bunch of Teds chasing a lone punk and I would run out of the shop cussing heavily in Jamaican to deflate the situation, as I could not bare to watch shit like that going down.

But at the same time if I saw a Ted being chased by a load of punks, I would have done the same thing.

One afternoon when I was behind the counter at Boy with Jeannette and Phil Strongman, this punk kid walked passed proudly waving his copy of "Anarchy in the UK" at us from the street. Little did he know that he was walking straight into a gang of Teds. One of the customers, Steve Roth, who looked like a real hardnut, but was as gentle as a butterfly— nutted one of the Teds, grabbed the kid and brought him into the shop. The Teds went mad—there were bottles and glass flying all over the place. As we tried to keep the door shut, Jeannette was busy turning coat hangers into weapons. The Teds eventually gave up and I chased them down the King's Road with a wooden mallet.

I got fed up working at Boy, so I went off to manage the Slits for a short while. The crucial four were Ari Up, Viv Albertine, Tessa Pollit and Palmolive. The evolution of the band was as fast and furious as the girls themselves. Viv and Palmolive, along with Keith Levene and Sid Vicious were in one of the earliest punk groups, the Flowers of Romance. Around the same time Tessa was going through the motions with the all-girl group the Castrators. Palmolive then teamed up with Ari, who was just fourteen at the time. I remember seeing them play one of their first gigs at the Roxy Harlesden (not to be confused with the legendary Roxy Club in Covent Garden). The line-up featured Tessa on bass and Kate Chorus on guitar. They were on the bill with Subway Sect, the Buzzcocks and the Clash: a punk line-up made in heaven. Shortly after, Kate Chorus moved on to form the Modettes making way for Viv Albertine to complete the original Slits line-up.

The Slits sound erupted as a stumbling rhythm packed with maximum energy and determination: Palmolive destroying the drums, Tessa's heavyweight bass with Viv's choppy guitar chords delivered like broken glass; on top of this raucous rhythm was Ari's signature screeching vocal style. They were rough, rugged and they rocked. These girls came with an attitude unlike anything I'd ever seen before, male or female! I filmed them countless times rehearsing, on tour and generally every time they played live—you just couldn't tell what might happen at a Slits gig (see *The Punk Rock Movie*). They soon gained a reputation for being unpredictable, chaotic and downright scary. But what intimidated the A&R men, inspired and empowered legions of young girls up and down the country who were fed up with the options open to them at that time.

The Clash were impressed enough to take them on the *White Riot* tour (Mick Jones would have to tune their guitars for them). It was at this point I realised that I was trying to manage the unmanageable. Bands fighting each other was one thing (and not unheard of) but the Slits would be fighting on stage, off stage, and all points in between. The thing about the Slits, they were the Slits twenty-four hours a day, not just while they were on stage performing. It wasn't an act. I remember trying to check the girls into a hotel one time, but before I'd even signed them in, we were being thrown out. Ari had decided to start wrecking the joint while we were still in reception. Such was the chaos that was the Slits.

John Peel could hear their potential and championed the band (listen to *The Peel Sessions*). Derek Jarman was so taken by their visual energy that he put them in his film *Jubilee* (they destroy a car). As for Malcolm McLaren, well he wanted to manage them and cast them as the female Sex Pistols. But these girls were nobody's puppets. I remember filming a Slits show at Ari's school in Holland Park (that's about the only way she'd attend) and predictably the gig ended in a near riot. It was mayhem. Someone let off a smoke bomb and kids were throwing butter and eggs. I was there trying to capture all this on film.

But it wasn't all outrage and chaos; these girls were breaking new ground without really trying. Musically, lyrically, stylistically everything was different. They were the last of the first wave of punk bands to get signed such was their reputation. They parted company with Palmolive (who ended up playing for the Raincoats) and she was replaced by Budgie (later of the Banshees and Creatures fame) with whom they'd record their first album in 1979, the classic *Cut*. The album was produced by the dub master himself Dennis Bovell (Matumbi/Janet Kay). Its sleeve featured the girls naked and covered in mud and the music inside was a sonic delight. Bored by what punk had become, the Slits were one of the first bands to embrace reggae, and later African rhythms. It was their love of reggae in particular that brought us together as friends. When we went to reggae clubs every eye in the house would be focused on Ari who'd be whipping up a storm on the dance-floor.

At this point, the notion of music video had started to emerge, and me and a guy called Mick Calvert realised that bands like the Slits were never going to get the sort of budget that other bands could get for a promo video, so we had the idea of getting ten grand from the record company and shooting a short film. The plan was that within it you could have a couple of promos and a half hour film. (The equivalent of the DVDs that get packaged with some CDs today.) Mick had come up through the scene in Bristol and had made a name for himself filming bands like the Pop Group. We went off and made a little film called *Slits Pictures*. If it had not been for us being into them, then this probably would have never happened—documentation of the Slits might not exist.

In 1980 with a new drummer (Bruce Smith, ex-Pop Group) they released the singles 'In The Beginning There Was Rhythm', 'Man Next Door' and 'Animal Space'. Next came the authorised bootleg *Retrospective*, an anthology of old studio tapes and early live tracks. They were constantly reassessing their sound, collaborating with the likes of the legendary jazz trumpeter Don Cherry, his step-daughter Neneh Cherry, Rip Rig and Panic, as well as reggae artist Prince Far I, all with Adrian Sherwood, who started the mighty On-U Sound label, at the controls.

At the end of the seventies there was a strong Bristol scene going on with Mark Stewart's band the Pop Group who merged dub reggae with punk, funk and avant-jazz. The Pop Group's music was like a bomb going off in your head and their songs, if you want to call them that, reflected their anti-fascist beliefs as well as Situationist philosophy. Their first single was "We Are All Prostitutes" with its flipside "A Report On British Army Torture Of Irish Prisoners" which says it all. Reggae stalwart Dennis Bovell produced their first album. Mark used to be a regular visitor to the King's Road buying fifties clothes before punk kicked in and it is said that he came up with the name the Pop Group travelling to London from Bristol to go to the Roxy. Later there were spin off bands like Rip Rig and Panic (named after a Roland Kirk album) who were experimenting with free jazz and avant-garde sloganeering.

By the late seventies, punk had become trapped by its own definition and post-punk bands like the Pop Group and PiL were actually far more liberating than what punk had become—a shambles of safety pins and bin-liner bands. As for the Slits, a new deal with CBS produced the *Return of the Giant Slits* album in 1981 and not long after, they announced their final gig at the Hammersmith Palais.

I remember taking Ari to a Twelve Tribes meeting in Kennington. The Twelve Tribes is basically the most mysterious school of Rasta thought, relating to the twelve different star signs and could be better described as a society within a religion. I do not know what possessed me to take Arianna from the Slits to this meeting. When I look back on the whole event, I must have been fucking crazy! The Rasta elders were there, and passed me the chalice and I passed it to Arianna. Worries! According to the fundamental aspects of Rastafari, just like most belief systems, giving the chalice to a woman was a no-no. I did not have this gender problem thing, Arianna was one of my brethren. There was a big argument about it and we were both kicked out of the building. Ari did not care then, and she does not care now.

Ari was confrontational when she was fifteen and is still like that today. I saw her a while ago at Metropolis Studios and James Brown was there. We went to the canteen to get some food and it had all gone. James Brown and his crew had eaten it all. Arianna went straight up to James Brown after he had left his table and said, "Oi you, you have eaten all my bloodclaat food." James just grunted, turned and looked at her.

Although never commercially successful, through sheer emotion and desire, the Slits created some great music and remain not only one of the most significant female punk-rock bands of the late 1970s, but had the potential to be one of the greatest female rock bands ever.

Madonna bow down, Courtney Love step back and as for Spice Girls—don't make me laugh. Whatever you think they've done, the Slits did it before…

15

THE PUNK ROCK MOVIE

"Movies will come—but none will have the brutal honesty of this remarkable documentary… Many of the bands are shown in a way that no film will ever capture again." Sunday Times on The Punk Rock Movie.

"Letts took full advantage of his opportunity. He shot punk as it should be shot, as Warhol or Pennebaker would have shot it." Time Out.

As soon as I had the camera I began filming the punks for practice. In my mind I had the idea of doing something like *The Harder They Come* one day. So, whilst I was filming the Clash play at Harlesden, somebody must have seen me. The following week I read in the *NME* that Don Letts was making a film about punk rock and I thought, "That's a good idea, I'll call it a film." Before long people were asking me when it was going to come out. I felt almost obliged to do it.

I knew that much could be gained from the blind "fuck you" energy of just going out there and doing it, without any

preconceived notions or value structures. I just started filming at the Roxy and initially I did not give too much thought
to the method. But the more I got into it, I started to question
the artistic process: What justifies you in picking up a camera
in the first place? Are you aware, deeply aware, of what con-
stitutes good picture composition and framing of your subject? Obviously I wasn't, but I did begin to take my new role
seriously.

After a while I began to think to myself, "This is not a
bad idea." I documented all the events that I thought were
either interesting or ridiculous. Consequently the movie was
representative of the whole movement. I was inspired to do it.
I approached the movie in the same way that punk rock had
evolved, saying, "Screw the rest of you, I am doing this the
way I want to." I was in the right place at the right time, and
looking back, I had a knack for filming what was important,
rather than tabloid punks trying to grab some screen time.

I ended up filming for four months and had to flog most
of my possessions to keep buying bloody film for my camera.
I didn't even read the instructions and could not afford a
microphone, so I rigged up this little mic I had lying around,
although I eventually bought a proper one when I got the
cash together. The whole thing had a life of its own—even
the title—it became *The Punk Rock Movie* because that's
what everybody was calling it.

After the shows at the Roxy, Chrissie Hynde, some of the
Slits, the Clash, Generation X and the Pistols would hang
out in Forest Hill, often all at the same time. One reason was
that they did not want the night to stop, they also wanted

to watch me putting *The Punk Rock Movie* together to check their moves on stage and get their shit together. If you look at the credits for the film, it says "scissors and Sellotape" and that's exactly what we used to edit the film. Jeannette and JR literally helped me stick it together. With Super-8 film you only had three-minute cassettes, so it was really fortunate for me that the punk bands seemed to cram everything into about 2½ minutes. Even when I spoke to them, most of the punks seemed to run out of things to say after about three minutes.

As the Roxy crowd knew and trusted me, I managed to film what the TV cameras couldn't get; the real background, the real truth. Every time someone announced that London Weekend were coming down to film, all the guys that were really important stayed away. The other kids stuck on some more safety pins and some more make-up and jumped around in front of the cameras—so it was a really distorted view of the whole thing. I managed to capture punk at its rawest and just at the right moment.

Journalists like Vivienne Goldman, Tony Parsons, Caroline Coon, Janet Street Porter and John Ingham were really influential in helping to break the punk rock movement—and they were also massive reggae fans. As well as pushing punk rock through the door, Vivienne and Caroline in particular gave me a leg up. I started to get a bit of a profile, bit of a vibe. Richard Williams of *Time Out* did a big write up on *The Punk Rock Movie* and put me on the cover. The Institute of Contemporary Arts in London then caught wind of the *Time Out* article and asked to show my film. *The Punk Rock*

Movie ended up running at the ICA for six weeks breaking all box office records. As I was using Super 8, there were no negatives, so I was showing the original in the cinema. It did not have any titles, it was just the raw film stuck together, a bit like the Fred Flintstone school of film-making. On any given night, the film would break or the bulb would blow. On several occasions I had to say, "Hold on everybody" and run up to Piccadilly to get a new bulb for the projector to start running the film again.

Eventually the film was blown up to 35mm and titles were added. I cringe when I see it now, as the techniques for blowing up film in those days were pretty primitive, but despite that there was a whole prestige about my film having a proper theatrical release. There were guys from the movie business telling me that it could be done, and I was thinking, "Here I am, a kid from Brixton, who am I to argue with them?" The end result blew it out of the context of punk rock. But although it works on the small screen, on the big screen it's torture for me to watch.

The movie starts and ends with the Pistols playing "God Save the Queen". I filmed the Slits at Sussex University, kids shooting speed in toilets and the self-mutilation. I caught the Sex Pistols at Screen on the Green and the Clash on their *White Riot* Tour. The film also included Johnny Thunders, X Ray Spex, Generation X, Siouxsie and the Banshees, Subway Sect, Jayne County and Shane MacGowan pogoing in his Union Jack jacket. There is no narrative, just pure punk mayhem. *Time Out* called the film "one of the top ten films of the year". Some of it was pretty raw; there's some guy slashing his stomach with a razor blade, Generation X are seen getting ready for their show in the dressing room and one of the band members flashes their cock in front of the camera, then there was Sid Vicious having a puff on a joint in the DJ booth at the Roxy. All this was interspersed with other footage of the time, like when I got busted at Boy for the window display.

There was always plenty to shoot at the Roxy; the theatrics of groups like Slaughter and the Dogs who'd come on stage covered in talcum powder. Then there were characters like Johnny Moped who looked like an extra from *One Flew Over the Cuckoo's Nest*. The Buzzcocks out of Manchester were one of my personal favourites, as well as the Adverts who featured the female bass player Gaye Advert. Dressed in black leather she was easy on the eyes and a favourite of the guys. I remember filming Eater (who had a twelve year-old drummer called Dee Generate) the night they decided to bring a pig's head on stage and proceed to hack it to pieces. Kids eh!

Later on, when Malcolm was getting a bit of press for *The Great Rock n' Roll Swindle*, an injunction was slapped on the showing of *The Punk Rock Movie*. Strangely I was not that bothered, because looking back I have never liked *The Punk Rock Movie* that much, as I could see how rough it was compared to the vision of what I felt I could do. Malcolm did me a kind of favour as I no longer had to show a film that technically made me cringe. It also gave the film a cult status. It's a bit like when I finally got to see the Stones' cult film *Cocksucker Blues* that never got released. The myth is sometimes better than the reality.

With me and Malcolm it was a David and Goliath thing. My film was a thorn in the side of a million dollar production. I have no problems with Malcolm. He has his faults, but who hasn't? Malcolm is very English and if you know what the English are about you can see it coming. I know that John Lydon and Malcolm understandably fell out big time, but I was never that closely involved with him to get burnt that badly, so I maintain a relationship with him. It cannot be denied that he always has an interesting spin on things.

I remember I had to get Sid Vicious to sign a form to give me permission to use footage of him in *The Punk Rock Movie*. Sid arrived with Nancy, and as usual they were pretty much out of it. He had a huge knife that he was prodding Nancy with. I told him to "chill with it" as someone was going to get hurt. Anyway, he signed the form and they left. Two weeks later, Nancy is dead. I have always thought that Sid did it, he was just the only one that didn't know it. Sid became a casualty and the poster boy of punk.

I went to a screening of *The Great Rock n'Roll Swindle* when it finally came out. Seeing John onstage in America in front of all those people was an emotional experience and it was sad to see the Pistols grinding to a halt in such a devastating way.

Martin Scorsese requested a private viewing of *The Punk Rock Movie* in London. So I went to meet him all fired up and excited. I managed to mumble about three words to him.

16

MALICE IN GANJA LAND

"It was getting too much to bear. We can't take it any more so we feel we have to hit back with something. Which is our music."

Big Youth, *Bass Culture*.

By 1978 Michael Manley was in charge of the People's National Party in Jamaica. They had won the General Election in 1976. Manley, a hardcore socialist, was a close friend of Fidel Castro and to gain public support and electoral success the PNP funded many of Jamaica's violent street gangs. The opposition, the Jamaican Labour Party, was without a doubt using similar tactics under the leadership of Edward Seaga. It is thought that one of the JLP's street gangs was responsible for shooting Bob Marley in December 1976 to prevent him from performing at the *Smile Jamaica* concert, for fear that his appearance would sway the vote towards Manley. This violent political culture, however, was not a recent invention. It had its roots in conflicts as early as the 1940s. It cannot be denied that the situation between Manley and Seaga did a great deal to provoke gun violence in Jamaica.

As Chris Blackwell had successfully built up his reggae roster with Island Records, Richard Branson wanted Virgin Records to have the same clout. John Lydon had been a guest on the *Tommy Vance Show* on London's Capital Radio and had chosen the playlist. Amongst his choices were tracks by Captain Beefheart, Can, Peter Hammill and John Cale. Lydon also showed his love of reggae by choosing Dr Alimantado's "Born for a Purpose", Fred Lock's "Walls" and Culture's "I'm not Ashamed". He also chose Augustus Pablo's "King Tubby Meets the Rockers Uptown" and Vivien Jackson and the Prophets' "Fire in Kingston". On the strength of this Branson asked Lydon to join him as an A&R scout on a trip to Jamaica to sign some talent for what would become the Front Line imprint of Virgin Records.

John invited me to go with him, so in February 1978 off we went to Jamaica. We were in trouble even before we got there. Obviously, I had never been to Jamaica in my whole life, the closest I had been was seeing *The Harder They Come*. I turned up at John's house with my passport, a plastic bag and one pair of underpants. When we got on the plane we did not realise it was a transfer flight via Miami. None of us had any visas and we were escorted by armed guard to the transfer plane. What did they think we were we going to do, invade Miami? It was a good few hours before we arrived in Jamaica.

Through the *The Harder They Come* and the music I had immersed myself in, I was pretty well prepared for Jamaica. It was not as much a culture shock as I thought, the Jamaican roots scene in the UK was really strong and it was only when I spoke they could tell where I was from, although the beads of sweat were a bit of a giveaway, not to mention my inability to walk on the scorching ground in bare feet. Apart from that, it was surprising how well equipped I was.

When we checked into the Sheraton Hotel we found out that Richard Branson had booked the whole floor. For John, life was a little strange; it was only weeks after the break up of the Sex Pistols. Malcolm had already started working on *The Great Rock n'Roll Swindle* and for John it was a chance to escape the paparazzi, although he still got hassled by them in Jamaica. We could be sitting around the pool and there would be some guy trying to take pictures with a telephoto lens. We ended up grabbing one of those guys and throwing him into the pool.

Over the next two weeks everybody who was anybody came by to try to get "some of the whiteman money" with the exception of Bob Marley (R.I.P), Bunny Wailer, Peter Tosh (R.I.P) and Burning Spear. Many an afternoon was spent pool-side hanging out with the likes of Prince Far I, I-Roy, the Gladiators, U-Roy, Big Youth and the Abyssinians to name a few.

Rastas were not supposed to be allowed into the hotel. In Jamaica at that time they were considered rebels, they were the voice of the people and they had a kind of "black power" doctrine which angered the local black upper- and middle-classes who were attempting to deny their blackness. The Rastas reminded them of where they had come from, and consequently were a definite no-no. It was only when Bob

Marley achieved respect throughout the rest of the world that the image of the Rasta was turned around. Because Branson was paying for it all, the hotel management turned a blind eye. The hotel staff were horrified because in those days it was almost illegal to openly show dreadlocks, consequently I wore mine under a hat.

All the mystical names that John and I had admired for years were now blagging food and drinks from us. Although we had imagined these artists to be big in their own town, the reality was quite different. Even though some of them had a huge cult following in the UK, more often than not, they would be seen as yet another hustler on the streets of Kingston, Jamaica who happened to have made a record for some unscrupulous producer.

One issue that caused major grief was the lobster. Part of the Rastas' doctrine was a set of dietary laws. No alcohol, tobacco, meat or shellfish. Anything that was not 'ital', the Rasta term that meant 'pure', was not allowed to be eaten.

I remember Prince Far I looking on disdainfully as John and I tucked into some lobster with melted butter. The hotel staff looked at me and said, "Rasta eat lobster!" and I replied, "Listen to my accent; I am an English dread, different culture." I had decided long ago that I would not blindly follow anything, having always found a degree of self-interpretation a necessity if I was to enjoy life and not be trapped by what I saw as dogma. Within a few days, Prince Far I had also learnt this lesson and could be seen sipping champagne with his lobster and fries by the hotel pool.

Punk had no impact on Jamaica other than the odd article in *The Gleaner* about a strange English phenomenon. But that didn't stop anyone looking at John and being more than appreciative of "the whiteman who sell 'nuff record, gold disc an' 'ting". One afternoon we ended up with Lee Perry in his studio where the assembled reggae artists had been hired to do reggae versions of "Anarchy in the UK" and "Holiday in the Sun". (Record companies? Who can figure them?). Jamaican musicians had become a little jaded since various Western artists had periodically arrived to jump on the reggae bandwagon. Consequently it wasn't about art or great ideas, these guys were making a living. You pay and they'll play. I can remember sitting in the smoke-filled control room listening to the cheesy reggae versions that Scratch's bunch of hired session men were banging out. Whilst drawing on the best herb that Branson's money could buy, John and I ended up giggling, not only at the absurdity of the scene, but also at the truly awful renditions of the music. Since the project was money-led it wasn't so much Dread at the Control, more like Bread at the Control.

One day I decided to try and visit a long-lost relative I'd never seen. John wanted to come along for the ride. And that's how I found myself riding in a huge white Cadillac with the ultimate punk, in search of my roots. The directions I had were crude to say the least—third bush on the left near where the Kentucky Chicken sign used to be...

We found ourselves in the back of nowhere amongst a few shacks scattered on a hillside. It was straight out of a Western, only with a Cadillac instead of a horse. After asking a few of the curious onlookers, I was directed to the right shack. After a nervous knock, an old lady emerged who I presumed was my grandmother. I quickly tried to break the ice by announcing, "It's me—your grandson from England." Maybe the words metamorphosed as they left my mouth into, "We wish you no harm, take me to your leader," because the old lady just stared at me as if paralysed. I quickly reassessed the situation, and decided that there had been some kind of information overload in the poor lady's head. Changing tactic, I told her that we were just gonna get something to eat. John and I made a hasty exit, dragging our chauffeur, who in the confusion had started loading up the trunk of the Caddy with various vegetables from the garden! Needless to say I never went back. It was sometime after that I realised how fazed the old lady must have been to see her dreadlocked grandson and Johnny Rotten arriving in a white Cadillac greeting her in the Queen's English.

It was on this same trip that I made the most embarrassing comment of my life. Through a mutual friend (Dickie Jobson, director of *Countryman*), John and myself found ourselves around Joni Mitchell's house in Jamaica. We're burning herb, as one does, when I burst out with, "What is this shit we're listening to? Take it off!" Joni calmly replies, "It's my new album, actually." Back-pedalling furiously (coolly disguised by the perennial shades) I foolishly reply, "Well it's not 'Carrie'." Pathetic—but for the life of me I couldn't think of a better comeback. John's giggling on the sofa didn't help.

John did not want to go back to London with a suntan, so he walked around in Jamaica's summer heat dressed in heavy black motorbike boots, black hat and heavy black woollen overcoat. He looked like Lee Van Cleef. The Rastas loved John. To them he was the Don of punk rock from London. They were aware of all the trouble he had stirred up in England, and they respected what he stood for and his rebel stance. John is Irish, and there is a definite connection between Jamaicans and Irish people. A strange example of this was the sign 'No Blacks, No Dogs, No Irish' (which John amended for the title of his autobiography) that used to appear in pub and lodging windows in fifties London.

John and I became friendly with U-Roy, another reggae legend—or the geezer with the best herb, as he soon became known to the two wide-boys from London. More often than not we were to be found giggling behind a cloud of smoke in U-Roy's backyard, and his posse were really impressed by John's apparent ever-expanding lungs as he could draw on the chalice along with the best of them. It has to be said, I was far more modest. One day we travelled out to 'country' with U-Roy's "Stur-Gav" sound system, a gargantuan mobile disco Jamaican-style, piled onto the back of two massive trucks. The numerous sound boys were hanging onto the equipment for dear life, because they all knew you could 'drop a bwoy but yu can't drop a box'.

We finally reached our destination after weaving our way through some truly glorious countryside, where John and I decided to burn some herb while the sound system was being strung up. The next thing I remember is being woken up and somebody saying, "We're ready."

"Ready for what?" I mumbled.

Above: My father, St. Ledger Letts, and his
Duke Letts Superstonic Sound System. *(Author archive)*

Above left: At home with my father, Brixton, 1960.
Above right: My mother Valerie Letts. *(Author archive)*
Below: The posse at Christchurch Primary School, Brixton. *(Author archive)*

Above left: Aged four. **Above right:** In my bedroom, Stockwell, 1969. *(Author archive)*
Below: In the living room, Stockwell, 1972. *(Author archive)*

Above: The Acme Attractions stall, King's Road, Chelsea. *(David Parkinson)*
Right: The Acme poster. *(Author archive)*

Smarten Up!
GENTLEMENS
CLOTHING
FROM
'Acme Attractions'

THE BASEMENT 'ANTIQUARIUS'
35 KINGS ROAD CHELSEA SW3

Above left and right: Acme Attractions. *(Sheila Rock)*

Left: Sid and Jeannette at Acme. *(Author archive)*

Right: The Forest Hill crew (l-r) Leo Williams, Jeannette Lee, myself, Janice, Margaret and JR. *(Author archive)*

Above: Jeannette Lee. *(Sheila Rock)*

Right: The South London Posse, 1975. *(Author archive)*

Opposite: Tappa Zukie, myself and Patti Smith onstage at the Hammersmith Odeon, 1975. *(JR)*

Opposite top: With Bob Marley, London, 1975. *(Author archive)*

Left: The iconic shot of me at the Notting Hill Riots, subsequently used for the cover of the *Blackmarket Clash* album. *(Rocco Redondo)*

Above: A typical confrontation with the police's interpretation of the all-powerful SUS laws in Portobello Road, 1979. *(Author archive)*

AT THE ROXY
.43 NEAL ST.
COVENT GARDEN.

SATURDAY 1st JAN '77
bar open 8pm - 2am

WITH THE CLASH

Above and opposite: 100 days at the Roxy Club, London. *(Author archive)*

Opposite top: In Jamaica with John Lydon for Virgin Records. *(Author archive)*
Left: The King's Road biker, 1975. *(David Parkinson)*
Above: Invite to John Lydon's famed Gunter Grove party. *(Author archive)*

Above: Cover of Mark P's *Sniffing Glue* magazine, February 1977. *(Author archive)*

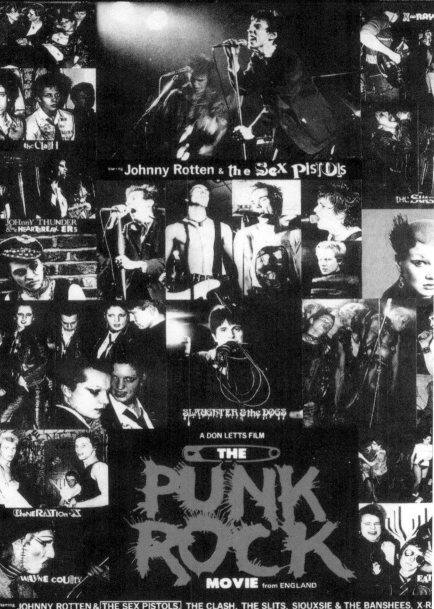

"The Sheer Blind Energy of What's Happening in the New Wave."
OBSERVER MAGAZINE

starring Johnny Rotten & the Sex Pistols

A DON LETTS FILM

THE
PUNK ROCK
MOVIE from ENGLAND

starring JOHNNY ROTTEN & THE SEX PISTOLS, THE CLASH, THE SLITS, SIOUXSIE & THE BANSHEES, X-RAY
SLAUGHTER & THE DOGS, GENERATION X, SUBWAY SECT, SHANE, WAYNE COUNTY, EATER
JOHNNY THUNDER & THE HEARTBREAKERS, ALTERNATIVE T.V. Produced by PETER CLIFTON Directed & Photographed b
Executive Producer Produced by Associate Producer ANDREW CZEZOWSKI Edited by Still Photography by
TER CLIFTON NOTTING HILL STUDIOS JOHN HACKNEY HUMPHRY MURRY & SHEILA ROCK A PUNK ROCK INC PRESENTATION In COLOR & 4 TRACK S

BLACK MUSIC & JAZZ REVIEW

TEMBER 1979
0p $1.75

LETT
MA
RANKI
MOVI

.B. KING
& QUEEN)

PYRO GYRA
HOTOSYNTHESIS

Opposite top: With Big Youth. *(Adrian Boot)*
Opposite bottom: With Kosmo Vinyl and Paul Simonon, 1977. *(Author archive)*

Above: At Wessex Studios with Joe Strummer. *(Pennie Smith)*
Below: Filming Joe Strummer in Battery Park, NYC. *(Bob Gruen)*

Above: During the Clash's residency at Bond's NYC. (l-r) Nina, myself, Rza, Futura 2000 and Fab 5 Freddie. *(Bob Gruen)* and the graff artists tags.
Below: With Africa Bambaataa. *(Author archive)*

Above: Andy Warhol, backstage at Shea Stadium. *(Bob Gruen)*

Left: Island Records founder Chris Blackwell, Washington DC. *(Author archive)*

Above: Daisy Lawrence, friend, Tricia Ronane, Audrey le la Peyre, Jet Letts. *(Author archive)*

Right: On the set of the "Rock the Casbah" video shoot in LA, early eighties. *(Author archive)*

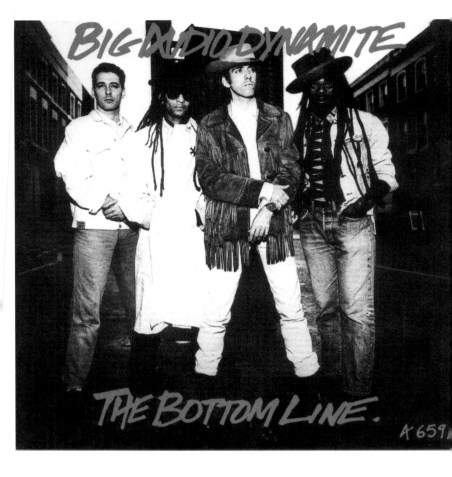

BIG AUDIO DYNAMITE

THE BOTTOM LINE.

A 659

B.A.D.

NO. 10, UPPING ST.

Above: Taken during the filming of the "Sightsee MC!" video. *(Jim Jarmusch)*
Below: Video shoot, LA, early eighties. *(Author archive)*

Above: On the set of the "Medicine Show" video shoot
with Joe Strummer, John Lydon and Paul Simonon. *(Adrian Boot)*
Below: With Federico Fellini. *(Author archive)*

Above left: With my wife, Grace. *(Author archive)*
Right: The Police Chief, Rio de Janeiro. *(Author archive)*
Below left and right: With Mick Jones, Big Audio Dynamite. *(Adrian Boot)*

Above: Big Audio Dynamite backstage. (l-r) Greg Roberts, Dave Stewart, Leo Williams (sitting), Don Letts, David Bowie, Jimmy Cliff, Mick Jones, Dan Donovan (sitting), Peter Frampton, Paul Simonon. *(Bob Gruen)*

Above: Namibia, 1991. *(Author archive)*
Opposite: The CD compilation albums.

SOCIAL CLASSICS VOLUME 2

DREAD MEETS PUNK ROCKERS UPTOWN

selected by DJ

DON LETTS

The soundtrack to London's legendary
Roxy Club December '76 – April '77

DON LETTS PRESENTS
THE MIGHTY
TROJAN
SOUND
Ds SELECTED FROM
E TROJAN VAULTS

Social
Classics
Vol 3
Dread meets
B-Boys downtown
The Hip Hop Sound Of New York '81-'82 as selected by Don Letts

Don Letts, London 2006. (Phil Fisk)

"Dance done," was the reply.

John and I had smoked and crashed out where we we'd been sitting, and that was six hours earlier!

As the trip progressed, while John was doing his stuff I hung around with my Super-8 camera. Back in those days, a black man with a camera was a big deal. An English dread with a camera was an even bigger deal.

One time Tappa Zukie took me and John to Rema, the heaviest part of Kingston—they used to call it "Jungle" and it was a no-go area for the police.

I was thinking, "What is the big deal, where are all the guns?"

This guy said, "Do you want to see a gun?" and reached into his back pocket and whipped out this massive fucking gun.

Suddenly there was all these guns about. Me and John were shitting ourselves. Three days later, the guy that had drawn his gun was dead.

As gun crime was so prevalent in Jamaica, Manley had this place built called Gun Court which was essentially a big fortress; a Stalag-type place. If you were caught with a gun, you were sent to Gun Court for indefinite detention. He had the building painted red, because he thought "red is dread" inspired by the Clint Eastwood film *High Plains Drifter* where he has the town painted red. Jamaica was a country into Westerns like no other, and consequently there were recording artists called Clint Eastwood, Gregory Peck, John Wayne and Dirty Harry. Jamaicans loved Westerns and Kung Fu—there was even an artist called Bruce Lee! There was a period when the gun thing got so out of hand, the rude boys would shoot at the screens in cinemas when certain movies were showing. The solution? They put up concrete screens.

One hot and sticky afternoon I decided to film the exterior of Gun Court and the next thing I knew, two soldiers grabbed me and marched me into a cell. It was like being in a concentration camp. The holding cell was a pit. I remember walking past it looking into the inmates' eyes and realising that they would never see freedom again. In the cell the guards told me, "You cannot film round here," and I replied in my best English to emphasise that I was a tourist.

They asked me, "How do we know you are from England?"

There I was with dreadlocks and they thought that anyone that came from England would be conforming by dressing like an Englishman.

I pleaded, "Listen to how I am speaking!"

They replied, "Hmmm, true, true."

They continued to question me, and came up with the bright idea of testing my knowledge of the UK by asking me where Durham Prison was! Eventually they convinced themselves that I was not local and after two hours they let me go. Sometimes I wondered whether the new generation of blacks in England like myself, who were empowering themselves by emulating their Jamaican brothers, were almost overdoing it.

For me it was a great experience; reggae had got me into the punks and the punks got me closer to the reggae acts. Consequently, I became very friendly with Prince Far I (R.I.P.), Tappa Zukie, I-Roy (R.I.P.), U-Roy and Big Youth. But the whole trip was a bit of a eye-opener for Virgin Records who went to Jamaica thinking that they would be dealing with clean-cut artists like the soul boys from America. People like Far-I and Keith Hudson (R.I.P) could be very scary if you caught them on a bad day. They had a different way of settling their business. Far I fell out with Branson. He later released a track on Adrian Sherwood's On-U Sound label called "Virgin" which included the words "Branson is a pickle with no place on my plate". I had played Far-I's "Deck of Cards" at the Roxy. His voice sounded like he had gargled with bleach. Guys like that were consummate rude boys. They were not bad people but they were tough. Him merely saying, "Good morning," in a heavy Jamaican dialect to the staff at the record company could sound really intimidating.

When we came back from Jamaica, Vivienne had boarded up the front of Seditionaries (another name change) and sprayed up all this stuff slagging John off for going to Jamaica. I decided to film a bit of it on my Super-8 camera and Vivienne came out of the shop and attacked me. I had to pin her to the wall to try and get her to chill out. Now a black man doing anything to a white woman on the streets was a dangerous move. I was shitting myself. I was not violent towards her, I was just trying to calm her down.

She has never spoken to me since then. I look back on that episode and laugh. I have no bad feelings towards her or Malcolm. They opened up my eyes to an alternative way. If they had not done so, God knows where I would be today.

17

WE ONLY WANTED TO BE LOVED

In 1978, after the break up of the Pistols, John Lydon returned with a new band, Public Image Limited. Lydon, Keith Levene, Jah Wobble and Jim Walker fused dub and rock into a warped, paranoid and claustrophobic sound. As long as I had known John, he had always been listening to reggae and avant-garde stuff like Can's *Tago Mago*, Curved Air and Tangerine Dream. All these elements came together with the early PiL tunes.

I had always moved between the Pistols and the Clash camps. Each camp was very separate. As much as the British punk scene is portrayed as a single entity, there was always one-upmanship and creative competitiveness between the bands. After the Pistols split, and John Lydon and I returned from Jamaica we became even closer, so I began to hang out with the newly-formed PiL. John told me that back in the Pistols days both Paul Cook and Steve Jones hadn't wanted to travel on the same tour bus as him as he continuously played my reggae compilation tapes.

Their first album, *Public Image* and its follow-up, the hugely influential *Metal Box*, had elements of a King Tubby mix style to them. For their first single "Public Image"—a vicious attack on media misrepresentation—they needed a promo video to accompany its release. My first venture into video was to be the antithesis of the cheesy narrative-driven style of film-making that was in vogue at the time. Before the PiL promo, I was Don Letts DJ at the Roxy, dread with a camera. All of a sudden I had a film crew and a 16mm camera. The promo was shot at a studio in Olympia and I was making the shit up as I went along having never been to film school.

The video suited PiL's mood, being totally anti-celebrity. It showed them playing in a dimly-lit studio. Because it was John's band, I naively decided people just wanted to see him. Due to my total inexperience I went for the safe option. It is just John's dynamics that give the video any substance whatsoever; it was a very intense and dark performance. Working with PiL was always tense as they were so volatile, but that in itself produced its own vibe. Then Wobble would just sit down and play these seismic bass lines! Pure madness!

Everyone in PiL was on different drugs. One person was up, one was down, one was coming in sideways. The initial optimism that they had soon turned dark. They were all coming in on very different wavelengths. Out of that chaos came those moments of brilliance with their music.

Some video-makers add a narrative to their work and I thought that was kind of stupid and limiting. What is great about music is that everyone has their own interpretation of what the songs are about. So I used to just throw in abstract images that kept the song open-ended. After shooting that PiL promo, I started to believe in myself, and think that I really could learn and progress as a film-maker.

Jeannette and I had been an item for a very important part of our lives, but around that time we split up. She had me crying on the street. I had introduced Jeannette to John, who then got her involved with PiL in very much the same way that Mick Jones later got me involved with Big Audio Dynamite. Neither of us could play musical instruments, but we had a huge musical knowledge. We both also had firm opinions. Jeannette could say bollocks to Strummer and Lydon and they would listen to her. She started managing PiL, eventually becoming a part of the band; she is even on the cover of their *Flowers of Romance* album. When Jeannette got involved with PiL, I was off in a huff.

Soon after, Keith Levene and Jah Wobble needed some money, so they ended up making a single for Virgin Records called *The Steel Leg vs The Electric Dread EP*. They got me down to the studio to work on some vocals, even though I had never sung in my life. I remember sitting on the stairs with a microphone trying to write some words.

Eventually I said to them, "OK guys, I'll go home and work out some lyrics."

I never heard back from them and the next thing I knew there was a record out. They had used my demo vocals and stuck them on the track, and put a picture on the cover of someone with a bag over their head. Suffice to say, I would not have done it if I had known that was going to happen. So everyone thinks the person on the record sleeve is me. I was pissed off.

I came up with the title "Haile Unlikely". I was messing around with this idea of "OK, I am black, but I do not want to go back to Africa." Essentially the lyrics questioned a return to Africa and the following of Selassie. It definitely caused some controversy amongst some Dreads who thought I should not be writing lyrics like that. I don't think Keith and Wobble fully appreciated that I was going out on a limb writing stuff like that. Basically I was saying, "Here I am, a young British Dread, and I ain't going nowhere mate! I'm not leaving. England is my home."

A lot of the brethren were like, "Don Letts, bloodclaat." It was a crap record and I look back and laugh about all this stuff now. The interesting part of that experience was that I had the bollocks to pick up a microphone and sing in the first place. It gave me the courage to do what I would do later on with Big Audio Dynamite and Screaming Target. One thing Jah Wobble said which has always stayed with me is, "You have to stand firm in this life, firm as a fuckin' tree man!"

Pil's headquarters was in Gunter Grove, Chelsea, where John Lydon lived. It was like the Addams Family house. He had a cat called Satan that he trained to fetch things for him. One time we were round there taking sulphate—it was cheaper than booze in those days. We were bored and started messing about, so I picked up a canister of lighter gas and sucked some of it in. Little did I know that I had inhaled a mixture of air and gas. Anyway, I lit it and BOOM. The whole room shook and all the hair on my face disappeared, my eyebrows included!

John had the whole house apart from the flat below. Those poor people living nearby must have been terrified. John's big speakers blasting out reggae all hours of the day must have really shook them up.

I would spend a lot of time there, as did the Forest Hill posse. I even took Dr Alimantado round to the flat to see John. After the physical and verbal abuse John was getting on the streets during the Pistols era, Alimantado became one of his heroes, and "Born For A Purpose" his anthem.

"If you feel like you have no reason for living, don't determine my life," sang Dr Alimantado on the classic track which he penned after a near-fatal "accident".

On Boxing Day 1976 the good Doctor was struck down and nearly killed by a bus while walking up Orange Street. He eventually recovered, and being penniless, he managed to get a free session at Channel One Studio where he recorded "Born For A Purpose". An emotional and uplifting song, it told the story of how the bus driver was intent on running him over for daring to wear his dreadlocks in the street: "You wilfully hit I down, and God take I up, he take I up." He could not have known how those lyrics would resonate with the first generation of British blacks. Wearing welders' shades, dreadlocks flashing, complete with three-piece suit and 'ting, this larger-than-life character was a major inspiration to yours truly.

"Born For A Purpose" also struck a chord with another group of UK rebels. In 1977, John Lydon, then Rotten, named it one of his top ten tunes of all time. The Clash would also later pay respect with the lyric "like the Doctor who's born for a purpose" on "Rudie Can't Fail" from *London Calling*. The track was written during the summer when Joe and Paul were going to a lot of reggae shebeens and blues dances, partaking in herb and brew and generally being turned on by West Indian culture. It was a great song, with Joe's description of the Rudie character who was "drinking brew for breakfast" and wore a "chicken skin suit".

Joe Strummer once told me that Dr Alimantado's "Poison Flour" was a tune that Paul Simonon played all the time, citing it as an example of how to sing about things that had an effect on daily lives. It was this reportage quality in the lyrics of 1970s reggae that captured the punks' imagination (along with the bass lines and the weed!).

So "Born for a Purpose" quickly became one of the few records to actually bridge the curious alliance that was punk and reggae during that period in the UK. I had the good fortune to strike up a relationship with the great man himself when we met in Daddy Kool, then London's premiere reggae shop managed by Steve Barrow, who now runs the Blood and Fire record label.

Dr Alimantado was known to drive around in a Mini delivering his tunes live, direct and personally to the handful of reggae shops in London. He even took a leaf out of the punks' DIY handbook, spray-painting graffiti about his latest releases all over town.

When you went round to Gunter Grove it was like a trial by fire. John would fuck with you. If you had a weakness, John would find it. It was almost like people were coming round for John's entertainment and would walk out of that place psychological wrecks. It was only those that could stand there and take it that John would let back in. Polystyrene from X-Ray Spex came round one evening, she was acting kind of weird and disappeared upstairs. Half an hour later she came back down, she had cut all her hair off. John and I were freaked and at that moment there was a knock on the door. It was her manager and literally two guys in white coats. She was going through a rough time and they took her away.

For Leo Williams' birthday (Basement 5, B.A.D, Dreadzone) John decided to throw a party at Gunter Grove. The two tribes were on the floor with their Red Stripe, sensi and the heaviest dub reggae courtesy of the John Lydon Sound System. I can remember the bemused look on John's face as he watched Althea and Donna, who were also in attendance, skank the night away. This was a "punky reggae party" before Bob Marley even penned the tune.

One night there was a police raid. John did not know what was going on, all he knew was someone had entered the flat. He ran down the stairs with a huge sword that someone had given him as a present. The police must have wondered what the fuck was happening. The police sniffer dog chased Satan, who climbed up onto the speaker in front of John's teapot where his weed was stashed. The police thought the dog was barking at the cat, and did not think any more of it. The cat had saved the day. John was taken down the cop shop, bare-footed in his dressing gown and pyjamas. He had to walk back down the Fulham Road and all the way back to

Gunter Grove dressed like that. He was seriously pissed off and moved to New York soon after.

18

BASEMENT 5 DUB VERSION

After the Pistols' demise, a huge number of diverse British bands sprung up really quickly, inspired by the notion that you didn't have to be a musical virtuoso or loaded with cash to get a foothold on the ladder. When clubs like the Roxy and the Vortex folded, more sprung up overnight and soon there were a multitude of venues for bands to play all over the country.

Around the same time, the dreads at Forest Hill and I got offered the job of cooking food at a reception for the reggae band Third World that Island Records was promoting. I realised that Chris Blackwell, who I'd never met, was going to be there. So me and the Rasta crew were in the kitchen cooking a Jamaican meal. Leo and JR did the cooking as I cannot cook for shit. But I could look good, so I put a chef's outfit on over my electric blue zoot suit.

When the food was ready I removed chef's outfit, went up to Chris Blackwell and introduced myself as Don Letts. I had a lot of front in those days. I asked Chris for some money so that I could start a band. I asked for fifteen hundred quid, which in my mind was a lot back then. I should have said fifteen thousand. He wrote something on a napkin and told me to take it to some geezer who gave me the money which I used to start the group Basement 5.

It was Leo Williams on bass, JR on guitar, Tony on drums and we got in a guy called Winston Fergus to sing. We lost Winston shortly after we got the gig supporting PiL at the Rainbow on Christmas Day 1978, and I stepped in—I didn't really want to, but we were getting gigs in places like Portugal.

I took Basement 5 to Island Records, seeing as it was Chris Blackwell that had given me the money. At that time the photographer Dennis Morris was working in the art department there and he eventually ended up singing for them.

For some strange reason Dennis decided one condition of the band being signed to Island Records was that I was not to be involved in any way. I did not want to sing anyway, but I was shocked to find out that Leo, JR and Tony all agreed—which hurt at the time. Years later Leo Williams and I would go on to join Big Audio Dynamite. We have actually known each other for over thirty years and remain the closest of friends.

Basement 5 was the only example in the UK of a black band being influenced by punk rather than the other way round. Again it was interesting to see a band doing something that was not classified by their colour or race.

All over the country things were happening. David Hinds put Steel Pulse together in the Handsworth area of Birmingham in 1974 with a backdrop of dole queues, police harassment and the collapse of British Leyland which mirrored what happened with the motor industry in Detroit. Steel Pulse was initially refused permission to play in Caribbean venues in the Midlands because of their Rastafarian beliefs. The link between punk and reggae brought them to the fore, and eventually they opened for Burning Spear, which brought them to the attention of Island Records. Their album *Handsworth Revolution* was a major landmark in the evolution of British reggae. They ended up supporting the Adverts, Generation X, the Stranglers and XTC and I have to say, blew their headliners off the stage every time. They became an important part of the Rock Against Racism movement and a punk favourite.

Black Slate and Ladbroke Grove's Aswad also started out at around about the same time. The Aswad that I loved was during their *Warrior Charge* era, but I did some film work for them later on when they were going through their populist phase. I think they found it hard sticking to their roots rock reggae rebellious stuff. (That is not just exclusive to Black music. If your music is anti-establishment and you have not got a catchy hook then you are going to have a hard time). They were not really getting their dues, so I can understand why they made the change that they did, although they lost their core audience and gained a new one.

On the UK reggae scene there was also Misty in Roots and Dennis Bovell with Matumbi who had been around since the start of the Seventies. Engineer and producer Dennis Bovell collaborated with I-Roy, Steel Pulse, Errol Dunkley and Johnny Clarke. He produced Janet Kay's massive hit "Silly Games" which kick-started Lovers Rock and was smoother than the reggae roots sound. Dennis and his group, called the Dub Band, also worked in partnership with Linton Kwesi Johnson on his albums.

As far as British reggae went there were some great records made, especially by Aswad, Steel Pulse, Delroy Washington and the Reggae Regulars. They had it rough, suffering from the "if you ain't from Jamaica then you are not real" attitude, which again was bullshit really.

The cultural interaction between reggae and punk was beginning to leave its mark on bands from both sides. Although musically punk drew more from reggae than reggae drew from punk, reggae would benefit from the increased exposure. The "anyone can do it" attitude also worked equally well in both camps.

19

RETURN OF THE SUPER-8

I have to say that it's not easy being a film-maker—especially when you're left of centre. Being black just increased the problems. During the late seventies interviewers used to say to me, "Aren't you doing well for a black man." I couldn't believe this attitude, countering with, "What the fuck are you talking about? I am a manifestation of my heritage and this is only the tip of the iceberg, dude."

When I started out as a film-maker there was no infrastructure for black film-makers. In the US directors like Spike Lee had a school of thought that he could tap into. He could look over his shoulder and there were people backing him up. I never felt like I had that here, I was totally on my own. Then there's that tokenism thing where only one black dude gets let through the door, but I was not fooled by that and have used it to get to where I wanted to go, rather than where people wanted to put me.

What *The Punk Rock Movie* was to punk, *Rankin' Movie* was to be for reggae. Linton Kwesi Johnson, Culture, Prince Hammer, Big Youth and many other reggae names were all in the film. I filmed Prince Far I playing at Dingwalls with his Chelsea FC bag that he claimed was filled with ganja, and there is some great footage of Dr Alimantado bursting into a full performance of "Born For A Purpose" in the middle of Daddy Kool's reggae shop. It was a Super-8 classic moment.

Rankin' Movie was not just about live performance, but also linking the youth of Jamaica and London. It juxtaposed footage of Jamaican police shaking down a car load of Rasta brethren in Kingston and footage of the Notting Hill riot in '76. I filmed U-Roy with his chalice and Tappa Zukie in Rema on his motorbike with the gun-toting brother who was shot dead a couple of weeks later.

Rankin' Movie ran at the ICA's *Britannia Waives the Rules* season in August 1979. Also shown was Menelik Shabaz's *Breaking Point*, which was about SUS brutality and featured a re-enactment of the occasion where the police beat up their own (black) community officer by accident. The Community Officer, after witnessing a fracas going on between the police and some black youth, stopped his car and tried to do the job he was getting paid to do. He ended up getting a beating from his fellow coppers.

There was no narrative to *Rankin' Movie*, it was a portrait of reggae culture. What held it together were the reggae performances. I had met people like Tappa Zukie and Prince Far I in Jamaica when I went with John Lydon, and they saw me as someone that could help them by putting them on celluloid. Up until that point there had been no visual documentation of them. I am glad I did it, as most of those guys have passed away.

Saying that, it was not premeditated, again it all happened organically. The film created quite a lot of publicity for me which helped significantly when I later approached Michael White with a script I had written called *Dread at the Controls*. The script was a modern reggae Western set in Brixton, centred around a mini-cab office. The cabs were the horses and the dreads were the cowboys. The script began at the cab office and ended with a race riot in London. *Dread at the Controls* captured the reality of black life in London. My script was directly inspired by Linton Kwesi Johnson's "Five Nights of Bleeding" which he recorded under the pseudonym of Poet & Roots. "Five Nights of Bleeding" really summed up life as a young black man growing up in the decaying and violent inner cities. The track came from a collaboration between LKJ and the dub master Dennis Bovell called *Dread Beat and Blood* which came out in '77. LKJ came to London from Jamaica in the sixties and was heavily into literature and poetry. He had two books published during the mid-seventies that helped put Jamaican language in print. He was also a reggae critic for the *NME* and was involved with the *Race Today* newspaper. LKJ's anti-establishment poetry went down well with the punk rockers and he remains a major inspiration of mine.

I worked directly with Linton a couple of times; the first was when he was about to release a new album, I realised that Island Records were not going to make a video. I went to Island HQ and got a grand with the plan to shoot a music video for him. I walked through a storage room and there was a huge ghetto blaster prop that was leftover from a Madness video. I looked at it and thought, "Well, if I drape a bit of black cloth over the middle bit, it would look like two speaker boxes. I also cut in some news footage, which was quite a novel idea at the time. So, Linton Kwesi Johnson got a video to promote *The Great Insurrection* album that opened up more doors for him, and I had yet another video under my belt, all for less than a grand.

Michael White bought my script and the film was going to be called *Dread*. In the end the film never got made, but it was kinda cool to think that the dread from Brixton came so close. We even got as far as casting the actors.

Around the same time Franco Rosso was making *Babylon*. It was about a South London sound system in late-seventies Britain called Ital Lion Sound System, and the people who passionately ran it against all the odds. Brinsley Forde, Aswad's singer and child actor, was in the film, as was comedian Mel Smith. Dennis Bovell provided the score and put together the soundtrack, utilising tracks like Aswad's mighty "Warrior Charge". *Babylon*, even though it was a great film, did not make that much money, so *Dread* was shelved. But hey, that sort of thing happens all the time with films. *Babylon* and Horace Ove's *Pressure* are two films that showed the black experience of living in Britain during the seventies. *Pressure* was shelved for almost three years by the BFI. Maybe this was due to the scenes of police brutality in the film. Ove had wanted to show that "black people were fighting for their rights under a very racist situation."

Opportunities for black British film-makers to break into the film industry back then were few and far between. There was Lionel Ngakane, who was born in South Africa and came to Britain in 1950 to escape the Apartheid regime. Ngakane was an actor, appearing in British TV shows like *Z Cars* and *Dixon of Dock Green*, who turned film maker. In 1962, he bought a 16mm camera and filmed and directed *Vukani-Awake*, about the struggle for South Africa's liberation. It was the first film about South Africa made by a black African. His second movie *Jemima & Johnny* was made in London in 1966 and became the first black British film to win an award at an international film festival. It depicted two children from different racial backgrounds who become friends in spite of their parents' prejudices.

There was also Lloyd Reckord who, like Lionel Ngakane, was another actor who turned to film directing. Reckord came from Jamaica to London to further his career in the theatre. He appeared in *Danger Man* during the early sixties and was still acting in the late 1990s. He made a short film called *Ten Bob in Winter* (1963) after he got a grant from the BFI. His film dealt with the issues of colour and class amongst Caribbean people. Against the odds, these pioneers laid a foundation for black British film-making, but it is a foundation that has been impossible to build on.

The only black British feature films to be made in the eighties were Horace Ove's *Playing Away*, and *Burning an Illusion* by Menelik Shabazz. Funding has always been a problem as there is this dumb perception that black films only appeal to black people. It is a chicken-and-egg situation. Black British films need to be marketed outside the black British community for them to do well in the box office, but until they become successful then the money men will not fund them. It is a very sad state of affairs. When the powers that be can see a bit of money in something then their attitude changes. In America it's not a black and white thing, it's a green thing. Then there is also that thing when they half let you through the door. Today black people dominate sports and the music world, but were we really put on this Earth just to entertain the rest of the planet?

20

CLASH CITY ROCKERS

I had seen the 101'ers with writer Chris Salewicz at the Elgin, but at that time I did not know Joe Strummer. The 101'ers were pigeonholed as being a pub rock band along with Dr Feelgood. It is said that to some extent it was the raw rock'n'roll sound of pub rock that paved the way for punk rock.

In 1976 the 101'ers released their debut single "Keys To Your Heart", which I played at the Roxy, but their album, *Elgin Avenue Breakdown* wasn't released until the start of the eighties. On the cover was this old black guy who I remember seeing around Portobello in the mid-seventies. He used to wear layers and layers of clothing and an army hat. I am pretty sure he was homeless. That guy was a west London fixture.

Out of the Clash guys, I got to know Paul Simonon first through our mutual love of reggae. We'd swap mix tapes, which was our way of communicating. A lot of white music neither related to myself nor my culture, but the Clash had grown up in my backyard. I could relate to their songs and they had some wicked reggae-style basslines.

Over the years Joe stole many of my reggae albums—you bastard Joe! I had tapes of Mikey's late night radio show in Jamaica called *Dread at the Controls*, which I lent to Paul. The show played reggae exclusively and whenever it was on in Jamaica the crime rate went down as it kept people off the streets. He championed "Uptown Top Ranking" by Althea and Donna. Mikey's knowledge, approach and experience of making reggae music was invaluable to the Clash during the *Sandanista!* sessions, and the end results of his contributions were stunning, with tracks like "Bankrobber" and "One More Time".

Evidence of the Clash's respect for reggae was seen before it was heard. Check out the "White Riot" picture sleeve. It resembles the cover of Joe Gibbs and the Professionals' *State of Emergency* album sleeve, where the band is lined up against a wall with their backs to the camera. People make quite a big deal out of the punky/reggae connection, but what were the Beatles and the Rolling Stones listening to? It was black music. It's just that to the uninitiated it was not that obvious within their music, but with the Clash it was right up front. It was in their lyrics, in their bass lines and their subject matter. Not only did the Clash cover Willi Williams' "Armagideon Time", Junior Murvin's "Police and Thieves" and Toots and the Maytals "Pressure Drop", they name checked Prince Far-I on "Clash City Rockers", Dr Alimantado on "Rudy Can't Fail", the Abyssinians "Sattamassaganna" on "Jimmy Jazz" and Dillinger, Leroy Smart, Ken Boothe and Delroy Wilson on "White Man In Hammersmith Palais".

It made me immensely proud that my culture was being represented by these guys instead of being lost within self-interpretation. With the Clash it was not white reggae; it was punk and reggae. Their songs brought some of their culture to my culture. Reggae spoke in a currency that the punks could identify with. It was the anti-fashion fashion, the rebel stance, and importantly the fact that reggae was a kind of musical reportage, talking about things that mattered. Songs like "Money in My Pocket", "I Need a Roof" and "Chant Down Babylon" struck an obvious chord with "the youth".

I think one of the advantages that I had when I started making the promos was that none of the bands that I worked with had aspirations of becoming actors or film-makers, of which the Clash were the best example. They just made music and let me get on with my job as film-maker. They were obviously aware of my work on *The Punk Rock Movie* and the PiL video, and chose me to be the man for the job.

The first video I shot for the Clash was "London Calling". The punk look was supposed to be about individuality but after the Bill Grundy episode with the Pistols very soon it became a uniform. The Clash and John Lydon were smart enough to see how it was putting them in a corner. Punk was supposed to be about freedom and liberation, and all of a sudden you had the "punk police" saying, "You cannot wear this, you cannot do that, you should sound like this."

The sound of *London Calling*, along with PiL, was the first real challenge to those punk shackles, throwing soul, reggae and rockabilly into the equation. It was cool seeing them break out of the restrictions that punk had very quickly developed. The Clash had also changed their look to an East End gangster style. They were always image-conscious rather than fashion conscious.

I was still learning as I went along, in my usual punk rock spirit. In those early days, videos or promos, or whatever you want to call them, were all built around effects—or worse, just nothing but effects. I was looking back further in time, to the old James Brown footage where the film was centred on stage with a couple of cameras locked on to capturing the performance and that really appealed to me. James Brown's performance alone was enough to hold you.

For "London Calling" we decided to shoot the video on a pier in Battersea on the River Thames. I'll admit it wasn't exactly a quantum leap of an idea as the lyric of the song is 'and I live by the river'! Back in those days shooting a performance outside was quite a big deal. I decided to have cameras on a boat to get the right angles. Naturally I did not know anything about tides. Actually I can't even swim, but then again I've never seen a fish walk! So when we got there to set up the cameras we found they were fifteen feet too low as the tide was out. There was also the current, so after setting each shot up we found that we were moving further and further away from the pier. By the time we had sorted out all these problems, it started to piss down with rain. Looking back on it now I'll have to admit that the rain really added something to the video. But after about three takes I just wanted to get out of there. Rasta man hates the rain and cold weather. I have not been on the Thames since. Johnny Green had set up the band's equipment in the morning and by the time the Clash turned up and were ready to go, Johnny had been on the pier for about ten hours—and then the rain started. At the end of the shoot, he'd had enough and chucked the monitor wedges into the Thames. The Clash thought it was hilarious as the speakers went floating off down the river. Needless to say, the monitors were hired and did not even belong to the band.

I am now told that the "London Calling" video is a classic. It was a textbook punk situation, turning your problems into assets.

By that stage the Clash had decided against playing large venues and were due to play at the Lewisham Odeon in South East London. I took the opportunity to shoot the "Bankrobber" video in the afternoon before the gig. Johnny Green and Topper's drum roadie, Baker, can be seen dressed in masks as villains running out of a bank on Lewisham High Street with bags of money. They are next seen spending the cash on Clash tickets at the Odeon. There is a sort of Ealing comedy feel to the footage. This was intercut with the Clash playing "Bankrobber" live at the Odeon with Mikey Dread at the controls. As I was filming the last shots of Baker and Green running to the back door of the Odeon, two police cars came round the corner with their sirens blazing. Armed police jumped out and had Baker, Green and myself pinned against the wall. Johnny Green told them that we were art students working on a project.

For the "Call Up", a song about dodging the draft, we originally wanted to shoot the video in a cemetery, but could not get permission from the local Council to do it. We had to think on our feet and ended up shooting at former sixties pop star Chris Farlowe's warehouse—which was full of military memorabilia and equipment as he was a renowned collector. The song was about registration for the draft in America— a subject dear to Mick Jones since he had attended a draft demonstration in New York. The setting for the video shoot was just perfect—another example of turning problems into assets.

In the aftermath of the initial punk explosion it looked like the major record companies had regained control and were having it all their own way. The Pistols had imploded, the Clash had finally signed to CBS after months of negotiations and I had reinvented myself as a film-maker. So it was a period of death and re-birth for all, and everyone looked to the Clash to take things to another level.

At this point they needed to progress, and so they set off to make their mark on America on the back of their *Sandinista!* album. I loved *Sandinista!* and still do. People still say it would make a great single album, but I disagree. I think it is fine being a triple album and it is very much a ganja album. Joe told me he was smoking so much herb he thought he was "turning into a tree at that time." It was a buzz for me to hear that dub and reggae were still at the heart of the Clash's music. After *London Calling* they could have continued on that rock'n'roll route, but they did not.

So in 1981 the Clash left for New York to do seven shows, and took me along to document the event on film—which became *Clash On Broadway*—and that's how this London-based Dread got to meet the B-Boys in downtown NYC. All seven shows were oversold, and the Clash ended up playing seventeen shows back-to-back to satisfy demand. The venue was smack bang in the middle of Manhattan, in a place called Bond's, Times Square. Before the Clash had got to New York, their "Magnificent Dance", a remix of "Magnificent Seven" was being played on the black radio station WBLS. The Sugarhill Gang's "Rappers Delight" was the first rap 12" to cross-over commercially. It was hearing this record that inspired Strummer to write "Magnificent Seven", which itself preceded Blondie's "Rapture" hit by several months and Grandmaster Flash's "Message" by two years. Frankie Crocker from WBLS had mixed a version of "Magnificent Dance" and over-dubbed bits of dialogue from the movie *Dirty Harry* with bits of *Bugs Bunny* samples. For the whole summer it seemed like WBLS rocked that tune and the B-Boys loved it. Mick Jones was responsible for bringing the whole New York hip-hop scene to the Clash. Check "Radio Clash", "Overpowered By Funk" and 1983's rarely heard "Escapades of Futura 2000". Hip-hop stayed with Mick right through to Big Audio Dynamite.

It was a musical form that the Clash took on board in the same way they had embraced reggae. In fact, much of what was released on Sugarhill Records left a mark on Strummer and Jones, and Sugarhill provided the blueprint for the birth of the hip-hop nation. I can't begin to explain the way it sounded when I first heard tracks like "The Adventures of Grandmaster Flash and the Wheels of Steel" as I was walking down 42nd Street. It was the perfect soundtrack to the mixture of excitement and danger, Hispanics and blacks, movie theatres showing Kung Fu or horror triple bills, checker cabs, ho's and dealers all fighting for space. Maybe if you played those tracks over the opening scene of *Taxi Driver* you might come close.

At that time, Times Square was an amalgam of drug pushers, prostitutes, muggers and break-dancers that hung around 24/7. Today Times Square is cleaned up and feels more like a bigger version of London's Piccadilly Circus, which is ironic now for a city they say never sleeps, because from my perspective it definitely takes naps. Further uptown was the Bronx, which is the only borough in New York geographically connected to mainland America, not that that did it any favours.

The Bronx has an interesting history. During the forties and fifties it was not the place of urban squalor that it came to be known as during the sixties and seventies. After the Second World War an influx of African-American and Latin immigrants settled there. They were happy with the formidable housing and wide streets. The beginning of the end was when work started on an expressway in 1959 that destroyed what was appealing about the area. People relocated, as did businesses and factories. By 1969, the expressway was finished and all that was left was the poor and burnt-out housing left by landlords fleecing their insurance companies. Crime, serious poverty and street gangs had a strong presence in the borough. Whilst the gangs waged turf wars, killing each other instead of fighting what was oppressing them, there was some respite with a gang called the Ghetto Brothers who were involved with community outreach programmes, as well as giving the drug dealers a hard time. The average family in the Bronx at that time had only $5,200 to live on per year if they were lucky. Cases of malnutrition and infant mortality were seriously high.

Despite all of this, there was a new sound breaking out of the badlands of the Bronx and Harlem, moving downtown via the New York trendies—and, it has to be said, with a little help from the Clash. They invited Grandmaster Flash, the Treacherous Three and the Sugarhill Gang to support them, aiming to turn downtown New York onto something that was going on in their own backyard. Initial reactions were not always favourable though; on one occasion the predominantly white audience threw bottles at Grandmaster Flash whilst they were on stage, little realising they were witnessing an embryonic scene that would soon dominate the world.

It was an exciting time, there had been the "punky reggae" thing in London and now there was that "punky hip-hop" interaction going on in NYC. The upcoming hip-hop and graffiti artists could relate to the whole punk vibe. It was like-minded people once again aligning themselves with the only rebel sounds around. Africa Bambaataa was particularly taken with punk rock, and later went on to do the "World Destruction" track with Lydon.

The hip-hop scene had roots in Jamaica, inspired by the rapping style of Jamaican toasters, which was ironic in itself, as the Jamaican DJs had been inspired by American jocks broadcasting out of Miami in the late fifties. The Bronx pioneer, Kool Herc, credited as being the "Father of Hip-Hop", and coining the term "B-Boy", was born in Jamaica. Herc adapted reggae's sound system culture and his twin decks were powered from lamp posts. The cops turned a blind-eye to Herc plugging into the NYC power supply as his block parties kept all the kids in one place and out of trouble. He inspired countless rappers and DJs. He brought the sound system to the table, Grandmaster Flash brought cuts and spin-backs, whilst scratching and the 'needle-pick up' was Grand Wizard Theodore's thing. Africa Bambaataa, who had been a member of a street gang, was known as the "Master of Records" as he had so many. Many ex-gang members became B-Boys. Herc and Bambaataa injected their creativity into the brutal ghetto.

While in NYC I was living downtown on Orchard Street with a guy called Peter Dougherty for a while and then in Spanish Harlem with Constantine. Peter and I had become friends in 1975 when the dub reggae I was playing in Acme caught his attention. We started trading tapes. I would give him stuff from my dub collection and he turned me onto stuff like Patti Smith, Ramones and Television. He also later sent me tapes from Harlem World and Disco Fever. Mick and I used to hang out at Gerb's apartment on St. Mark's Place where all the graff artists would meet up. He was like a big brother and guru to all the young writers and really looked after us all—me, Mick, Jeannette, Haze, Futura 2000, Dhondi (R.I.P), Zephyr, Obdewl X (R.I.P) and Fab 5 Freddy. It was another cultural exchange, understanding our differences brought us closer together, just like the old days when all the punks used to hang out at my flat in Forest Hill after the Roxy gigs.

It was Fab Five Freddy that took Debbie Harry to hip-hop events, much in the same way that I had taken Lydon and Strummer to reggae sessions during the seventies. Blondie's "Rapture" was probably the first 'rap' the masses got to hear, whilst Malcolm McLaren's "Buffalo Gals" video introduced the world to the look and moves of the scene. It is said that Bambaataa was wearing a *Never Mind the Bollocks* T-shirt when Malcolm first saw him across a street in New York. Bambaataa had a vision of bridging punk and hip-hop, and the black youth thought he was crazy, which was a similar reaction I had from my Rasta brethren before going off to play reggae and dub at the Roxy a few years earlier.

By the mid-seventies, the hip-hop scene was well on its way to being established in the Bronx and Harlem in Disco Fever and Harlem World. During my stay in New York the scene migrated downtown to The Roxy via Club Negril.

Club Negril was one of the first downtown clubs to embrace the emerging phenomenon. Located on 2nd Avenue, between 11th and 12th Streets, the club had one of the best sound systems in New York and featured cutting-edge underground reggae and dub, so much that Bob Marley used to visit whenever he was in New York. In 1981, Rza Blue came to New York for a two week holiday from London. She bumped into someone that worked for Malcolm McLaren and Vivienne Westwood, then ended up managing and representing their fashion empire in New York. Rza used to frequent Club Negril and persuaded the owner to let her put on a club night of her own. Naturally I checked the club out, as did the Clash, and PiL who were now living in N.Y.C .

Eventually Rza wanted to put on something new and different to the usual dub and reggae nights. Malcolm had Bow Wow Wow playing at the Ritz. Supporting them was Afrika Bambaataa and the Rock Steady Crew who used to have the philosophy that, "It does not matter if you're black, white, Spanish, Chinese, or anything. It depends on who you enjoy dancing with and how you respect each other." Rza was blown away by what she saw and persuaded both Afrika Bambaataa and the Rock Steady Crew to perform at Club Negril. Rza was quite clever with her PR approach. She knew that to break Bambaataa and Co downtown was not going to be easy, so she put on the flyers that the Clash were going to be the guest DJs. Well, they were not, but when the crowds poured in they were able to witness Bambaataa and the crew in action and went home happy anyway. Saying that, I do remember that Kosmo Vinyl from the Clash camp did DJ with Bambaataa on at least one night.

The evenings and club nights that Rza organised and ran were called "Wheels of Steel", and Rock Steady's manager, Michael Holman, supplied the talent to her. The first few nights were a bit tentative. She had *The Great Rock n' Roll Swindle* showing before DJ sets by Jazzy Jay, but it soon took off. Negril managed to remain underground and was nothing like the downtown disco clubs. I can remember the energy being electric. Bambaataa premiered Babe Ruth's "The Mexican" track there. Rza's nights were a great success as the white folk were unlikely to travel into any of the black areas of New York to hear or see the new talent. Members of what later became the Beastie Boys and Public Enemy could be found at Negril. It was just like the Roxy had been in London, but instead of bands playing, people would do their thing to the records, spraying up canvases and breakdancing.

Club Negril soon attracted people from every borough and engendered a cultural diversity that had been missing up to that point. Rick Rubin met Russell Simmons in this creative cultural climate and would soon take hip-hop to the masses with Def Jam.

Word quickly spread and the scene soon outgrew the small, dingy basement club, so after a short while Rza had to find another venue due to fire restrictions. After a brief stint on one floor of Danceteria, she found a giant skating rink called—surprise, surprise—the Roxy, and from there the scene really grew. Soulsonic Force, Run DMC and Kurtis Blow all played there. The writers would be painting on big canvasses while the DJs spun, and the B-Boys did their thing. Bronx, Queens and Harlem were all in the house, along with the kids that loved the culture. Like punk, hip-hop had become a complete sub-culture with its own dress code, film-makers, artists and photographers. The notoriety and popularity of the graff writers grew with the music and swiftly became more politicised. The East Village walls rapidly became giant canvases on which the writers could establish themselves. It wasn't long before the writing on the wall was being featured in the *New York Post*.

By the time I left New York, the Roxy was firing. It was the place to be. Jagger and Madonna were down there, mixing it up with street guys from Brooklyn and Harlem. But more than anything, it was great to see people at last coming together over this new music.

I can remember going to an outdoor event staged at the Lincoln Center in the middle of Manhattan, a break-dance competition between the Rock Steady Crew and the Dynamic Rockers with Rammellzee as compère. It seemed like the whole of the Bronx had invaded Manhattan. Thousands of black and Hispanic B-Boys and fly-girls dressed to impress. We're talking fat laces, Adidas shell-toe trainers, Kangols and those funny Italian glasses without the lenses. Symbols of cultural and social identities were manifested in articles of clothing and accessories. Some of the B-Boys stuffed their Kangol hats with plastic bags to get the same "puffy aesthetic" as the dreads had with their headgear. Talk about cultural pick'n'mix. If you were unlucky enough to end up in jail at Rikers Island or anywhere else, laces and belts were regarded as weapons, so they were removed. That is where the saggy and baggy jean and no laces look came from. The clothing styles of outlaw gangs, mobsters, pimps, sports celebrities, actors and martial artists were also thrown into the equation as the B-Boys and B-Girls customised their sneakers to give them their own identity. For most, funds were tight and they had no choice to do anything but mix-and-match to create their own unique style of dress. As with any burgeoning scene, the DIY ethic was evident right across hip-hop.

The atmosphere at the Lincoln Center was tense. The competition was chaos with the judges unable to see because the circle of youths were taunting whoever was doing their thing on the floor. All I could see were sneakers spinning in the air. The judges eventually gave up and the Rock Steady Crew won by crowd noise. After the show there were some smashed windows and a few hot dog stands pushed over, but it was amazing to witness such an event. That day hip-hop and B-Boy culture really made its presence felt in Manhattan.

Another defining moment was when Patti Astor (who had a lead part in Charlie Ahearn's 1982 hip-hop film, *Wild Style*), started the Fun Gallery for the graffiti writers to exhibit their works, which were becoming both famous and infamous (NYC mayor Ed Koch wasn't impressed by this particular art form). The Gallery put on shows that attracted old- and new-school writers, like Phase 2, Lee, Iz the Wiz, Lady Pink—not forgetting Obdewl X (aka Kiely Jenkins) and Kenny Scharf who were really sculptors that the graff writers dug. Lee, star of *Wild Style*, was very much like his Zorro character in the movie, always moving on his own. But you gotta love a guy that dedicates all his pieces to his mom. Within a year, two particular writers who showed at the Fun Gallery went mega: Keith Haring (RIP) and Jean-Michel Basquiat (RIP).

These events were interesting as you'd could see some of the old guard like Johnny Thunders (RIP) and David Johansen hanging around as well. What with myself, Lydon, Jeannette and the Clash in the mix, it was just like being in London in 1976 when punk rock was about to kick off; but this time it was hip-hop.

The Clash financed *Clash on Broadway* from the proceeds of their New York shows. The Clash dealt with reality and did not just take from their fans, they gave them something in return. They were down-to-earth guys and I enjoyed working with them. They were into disseminating information and therefore did not want *Clash on Broadway* to be just about them, they also wanted it to be about the city, using it as a visual backdrop to what they were doing. So during the day and after the Bonds shows we went out discovering New York. Not the postcard New York, but the underbelly of the city.

Whether it was Joe talking to some scat singer on a street corner or Mick getting engrossed by the whole hip-hop thing, or going to Coney Island beach to watch the sun coming up. The "Radio Clash" video was cut out of the *Clash on Broadway* footage. A few years later after seeing the video at a film festival Federico Fellini said that I "have the vision of a terrorist". He was smiling at the time, so I guess it was a compliment. Sounded great in Italian!

Topper was always off doing his thing which is now public knowledge. I remember trying to film him one night and all I could get was a conversation with him in the back of a cab on the way to him getting sorted. It was the only way to get him to talk. Topper eventually got the boot from the Clash and was not happy to be featured in the film so it was put on ice.

Not surprisingly, as the Clash were grabbing the headlines, people were falling over to show you what the city had to offer. And back then there was a lot on offer—why do you think they named it twice? It was like a rock'n'roll circus. I was working on the film, hanging out with the Clash guys and getting into clubs for nothing—thanks Howie (RIP). I'd spent my life enamoured with Americana, but now I was not watching it on TV, I was actually walking down 42nd street. What a trip!

As for the film, Bernard Rhodes put it into a lab in NYC, did not pay the bill, and after a few years the lab destroyed the negatives… Amongst the scenes that were lost was some film of Paul getting tattooed and Futura 2000 being interviewed with graffed-up subway trains passing by in the background. Along with some weird footage of Prince Charles' visit to New York there was also a scene of the Clash discussing the irony of their situation under the Brooklyn Bridge one night.

For the time that the Clash was in New York it seemed to me that they basically ran the gaff. People like Scorsese and De Niro showed up at the gigs. De Niro was doing *King of Comedy* at that time and invited us to visit the set. Scorsese asked the Clash to do a guest spot in the film; they are credited as 'street scum'. When I went to see the film on its release I remember seeing my name going passed in the credits. I was not even in the movie! It turned out that the Clash had this black bodyguard called Ray Jordan and they must have thought it was me—talk about subliminal. So I got a credit in a Martin Scorsese film and he spelled my name wrong. It says Dom Letts. Still, I was touched by having a 'credit'.

While I was editing *Clash on Broadway*, Charlie Ahearn was working on *Wild Style* in the editing suite next door. I remember going to see the final scenes of the film being shot at the amphitheatre and that was a trip. It was like a scene from *The Warriors*, but with a better soundtrack and everyone there was not an extra, but real. The movie documented the language, style, moves and attitude of hip-hop. It was sim-

ilar to punk, it seemed to be a reaction against the over-pro-
duced music coming out of the US at that time, which seemed
far removed from the harsh realities of life in the Bronx. As
always, it seemed that the people with nothing were coming
up with the most interesting ideas.

The Clash always had this thing about keeping their
shows culturally interesting, so they had people like Grandmaster Flash supporting them or Mikey Dread or Lee Perry
or Allen Ginsberg reading his poetry, which Paul was not too
mad about from what I remember. A lot of that came from the
influence of Bernard Rhodes, the Clash's manager. The Clash
were nobody's fools, Bernard was not the puppet master, but
his knowledge of the underground cultures that went before
definitely gave the Clash more depth. They could see the tradition that they were following, and they made music as a
way of communicating ideas as a protest thing, rather than
just having an agenda of making music to just sell records.
The Clash's audience in New York was a white rock audience.
Some of these people were not ready for a musical education.
Their impression of black music in America at that time was
the Commodores, Earth Wind and Fire and disco as that
was the only black music that got airplay; none of which they
were interested in. The music was not saying anything to the
people that were living and experiencing life on the streets
of the Bronx and Harlem. It was the equivalent of what rock
music had been to my mates pre-punk in London. So when
Grandmaster Flash came on stage only to be pelted with bottles, I remember Mick having to go out and say, "How dare

you? Not only are you disrespecting our guests, you're fucking disrespecting us too."

From NYC we moved on to Texas. Picture the scene: A dread filming an armadillo, an Arab guy, a Jewish guy and a limousine with huge cow horns. It was the most talked about thing in Texas that week. I had gone there with the Clash to shoot the "Rock the Casbah" video and we came up with this half-baked idea of Jews and Arabs getting along, which I thought was a brave move for the Clash considering what could be shown on MTV and what couldn't. The plan was for the band to be filmed playing in front of an oil derry, and I was amazed when Mick walked onto the set wearing these red long johns and black DM boots. Mick was pissed off about something that day, so I pulled him to one side and said, "Look Mick, you look like a matchstick, and don't forget film lasts forever, so if you look like a cunt today, you'll look like one forever." Mick got changed.

The Clash were like four sticks of dynamite. On the cue of "ACTION" these guys just went off. The armadillo was the mascot of Texas and was added for a bit of humour. Most people there had never seen a live one; only dead as ashtrays or handbags. For the scenes with the armadillo I had to crawl on my hands and knees backwards blowing at it to get it to walk towards the camera. The whole video was quite humorous; there is a scene where the Arab is driving the Cadillac and making the Jew pay for the oil. The video is a juxtaposition of ideas and thought-provoking scenes. The song itself was later used by the US military in the first Gulf War as a rallying cry. A prime example of left wing political statements being hijacked, distorted and completely misunderstood.

In the summer of 1982, the Clash played Shea Stadium supporting The Who, which is where I filmed the video for "Should I Stay or Should I Go". Whenever The Who came out of their dressing room everyone had to back off about thirty yards or something, it was fucking ridiculous! And they would not let the Clash have as much sound volume on stage as them either. We were backstage and Andy Warhol was there. I remember jokingly telling Warhol that there was acid in the cake, and the poor guy completely flipped out. I felt really bad about that.

Living in New York for that short time was great. Everywhere you went there was black music, rock music or Hispanic music all fighting for space. It was such a buzz. You could step out onto the pavement at 3.00 am and it was more like six in the evening. It was such a trip!

Recently I put together a CD compilation called *Dread Meets B-Boys Downtown*. Digging back I traced influential and less obvious tracks. So tracks like "Apache" by Michael Viners' Incredible Bongo Band from 1968, "The Mexican" by Babe Ruth from 1972 are alongside Kraftwerk's "Metal on Metal" from 1977. There are also tracks from the *Wild Style* soundtrack, the Fearless Four, Grand Wizard Theodore and the Clash's "Outside Broadcast", one of the rarer re-mixes of "Radio Clash". It's the soundtrack to my year in NYC.

21

CHOCOLATE CITY GO-GO

In the aftermath of Martin Luther King's assassination, the riots of 1968 pretty much destroyed Washington. Thousands of buildings and shops had been burned to the ground and as a result thousands of jobs were lost and insurance rates soared. The lucky residents that could escape did and fled to suburban areas. The unlucky that stayed behind had crime, grime and property values hitting rock bottom to contend with. In some areas the rubble remained there for three decades after the riots, and within this ghettoised state Go-Go was born. Created in 'The Chocolate City' (Washington D.C.), Go-Go was truly a live experience with the most happening club action I've ever witnessed—period.

Washington was very polarised. You could see the White House from the projects and poorer areas. The areas surrounding the White House were fucking unbelievable. When people do not have much, they look for an easy way out and drugs and alcohol often come into play, but so does creativity.

Chris Blackwell asked me to direct the music sequences for a new film he was producing with Maxx Kidd of TTED Records called *Good to Go*. The film was Chris's way of trying to take Go-Go global, in the same way that *The Harder They Come* had introduced many to reggae. Well that was the plan, but Go-Go did not translate well to film, which is not a put-down; if anything it is praise because there is something about it that is intangible. It was almost too hot for vinyl and definitely too hot for celluloid.

The original intention was for me to direct *Good to Go*, but Audrey, who I had met a year previously, was pregnant with my first son, Jet. We had my daughter Amber seven years later. Anyway, to cut a long story short I ended up working second unit filming all the live performances of Trouble Funk, Chuck Brown and Redds & the Boys. The movie starred Art Garfunkel and Harris Yulin and was about a Washington street gang called the Wrecking Crew who kill a woman when they are turned away from a Go-Go club. The police put pressure on Blass (Garfunkel), a burned-out reporter, to give Go-Go a bad name after he witnesses the brutal murder.

Chuck Brown was the catalyst for the scene that emerged in DC. He was the godfather of Go-Go (check "We Need Some Money"). His band, Chuck Brown & the Soul Searchers, had made a few fairly successful records during the seventies and their beat on "Ashley's Roach Clip" was later sampled by Eric B and Rakim and Soul II Soul. Brown came up with a new playing style that later transformed into Go-Go. As a musician, Brown became aware that clubs were booking more DJs than bands, and he had to do something about it. He noticed that people on the dance-floors did not like the pauses between records, so he worked out a way for his band to play whole sets without stopping, one song continuing into the next. George Clinton and guys like Isaac Hayes had stretched their grooves out to ten or fifteen minutes, but Brown managed to stretch his out for two hours and the crowds loved it.

Go-Go was the precursor of swing beat—that percussive groove, horns, drums and congas—it sacrificed structure and slick production to create a loose sound that oozed a community vibe. It was driven by a distinctive chanting vocal style coupled with 'call-and-response', firing lines back and forth between the audience and the group. Since many of the bands had ten or more members, the sound was 'phat'. A cranking horn section was another key feature. Many of the players started in school marching bands that provided music lessons and more importantly, free instruments.

Go-Go emerged during DC's most violent period, when it was named the nation's murder capital. The scene started to grow in the late-seventies and early-eighties, championed by Trouble Funk, EU and Rare Essence. Pretty rapidly interaction between the Bronx hip-hop crowd and the DC Go-Go crowd began. Kurtis Blow collaborated with EU, and Grandmaster Flash and the Furious Five covered "Pump Me Up" by Trouble Funk. The influence spread rapidly; in the mid-eighties Rick Rubin produced the Junk Yard Band's "Sardines", Spike Lee featured EU's "Da Butt" in his movie *School Daze* whilst Grace Jones was to feature EU on her hit "Slave to the Rhythm" and there was also DJ Kool's "Let Me Clear My Throat" released in the early nineties.

Venues like Washington Coliseum and the D.C. Armoury provided the location for these showdowns. Thousands moving, girls grooving, sweat dripping, let's just say you had to be there.

With the Go-Go scene came Angel Dust and that caused a few problems on the fringes. Go-Go was the ultimate black tribal rebel sound in Washington, home of the White House and the capital of America. People tried to demonise the whole scene saying it was all about drugs, but in reality that was only a small part of it. Go-Go was not played that much outside the Washington clubs, the scene was so of its time and its place that it never managed to break out of its environment during the mid eighties, but its legacy is all over Swing-beat and hip-hop.

The bottom line is: you don't know the complete story of contemporary black music if you don't know Go-Go.

22

THIS WAS
BIG AUDIO DYNAMITE

"Big Audio Dynamite were a riotous update of Clash City politics, movie sensibility and dubbed-up dance grooves with Mick's innate sense of true rock'n'roll still shining through his guitar playing." Kris Needs

May 1983. I was working on *Good to Go* in Washington whilst Mick Jones was playing with the Clash in San Bernardino, California. Topper had already been fired and Mick was the next to go. People talk about the Clash's demise as a bad thing, but I saw it as being inevitable. The parting was exactly the way it was supposed to be. I have always had a theory that there is a creative lifespan of about seven years for most bands, which is about as long as musicians can stand working with each other before they feel the need to move on and grow as individuals. It was exactly that with the Clash. If they had patted each other on the back, shook hands and wished each other well when they split up, then there would not have been anything going on in the first place. It was all because they had immense passion.

Whilst Paul Simonon had brought reggae to the Clash, Mick was responsible for bringing the New York beats into the equation. The B.A.D. sound was a progression that went beyond the elements of *Sandinista!* and *Combat Rock*. With B.A.D., my sampling was only ever the salt and pepper on the main meal. I can't take too much credit, my samples would only make up part of the garnish. Mick is an unbelievable tunesmith and producer. I have seen him throw away ideas that people could make albums out of. Mick had also mastered the trick of triple-tracking his voice across the stereo range, something he used to good effect on B.A.D. songs.

Mick initially put together a band called TRAC, with my friend Leo Williams on bass and Topper on drums. Tops wasn't around for long.

I can remember hanging out with Mick and Leo at a club one night. Mick looked to his left and there was Leo, to his right was me, and he said that he thought we looked like a band. There and then Mick asked me to join. I immediately told him that I could not play anything, and he simply replied, "Just remember Paul Simonon. He could not play bass when he joined the Clash." We auditioned for a drummer in the *NME*. That is how we got Greg Roberts.

The band was initially going to be called Real Westway, but Mick really wanted to use the name B.A.D. for the new group. He had been helping his old friend Tony James with sound mixing at the time and Yana, who was Sigue Sigue Sputnik's FX lady, suggested the name Big Audio Dynamite.

Initially I found it quite daunting, because all these guys could play instruments. I was desperately trying to find my own space in the band, so I threw myself into writing lyrics, which I approached the same way as doing a video. Whilst it was great to collaborate with Mick and I found him easy to work with, I was always conscious of the shadow of his previous songwriting partner, Joe Strummer, cast over me.

Mick gave me a Harmonix sampler and I started capturing sounds and dialogue from movies to give the songs a visual quality. I ended up co-writing a lot of the songs with Mick as well as working on the samples. Mick once described the B.A.D. sound as being "dance rhythms with a rock'n'roll guitar." The B.A.D. philosophy was to utilise all the elements of the media to create a fuller sound.

It was not just about making music, it was about ideas. I used to sit there and watch films endlessly while we were recording—we had film festivals in the studio while we made all of our albums. I watched movies with the intent of using bits of dialogue. None of us had any interest in making mega-budget rock'n'roll. Big Audio Dynamite had a wide-screen approach to making music. The only example of someone doing it before us that I can think of is Brian Eno and David Byrne's *My Life in the Bush of Ghosts* album.

Our first UK gigs took place in 1984 where we showcased rough songs that were still being worked on like "Strike", "Nation", and "Interaction". We also played an early version of what would be our first single, "The Bottom Line". We had

Leo Williams on bass, and Greg Roberts on drums, and we can't forget Mick's guitar roadie, Adam "Flea" Newman on "dynamite". Big Audio Dynamite was primed for action. Our sound was a blend of New York beats, Jamaican basslines, English rock'n'roll and me taking care of the sampled dialogue and movie stuff.

Dan Donovan who joined later brought in more ideas when he became our keyboard player. He was introduced to us through Tricia Ronane, now Paul Simonon's wife, when B.A.D. needed a photo. Although we were managed by Gary Kurfirst (Ramones, Blondie, Talking Heads) he was based in New York. It was Trish that managed us in his absence. Well that's how it felt. Besides she was much better looking than Gary and had a South London girl's attitude, a deadly combination. For the first album sleeve Dan was the photographer. While we were doing the shoot, Mick mentioned that he was looking for a keyboard player and Dan told him that he could play keyboards. He did not immediately join the group, but used to hang out with us and did the artwork. Mick eventually asked him to come down to the studio to play keyboards on the album.

As a kid Dan had studied classical piano for ten years so he came down to play on the record and basically winged it. The album had been written almost a year before Dan got there, so the music was quite locked down. We were all sitting around the studio listening to playbacks and Dan presented a mock up of the photo for the first B.A.D. single, "Bottom Line". Mick pointed at the picture and said, "There is a space for you there," and he was in the band. He helped turn "E=MC²" into a hit.

We were really tuned into what was happening at the cutting edge, we even ran a club called Planet B.A.D. on Kensington High Street, and we were very much a self-contained band, between us we had each different department covered. I did all the videos and Dan Donovan did the photography and artwork, and we also had a very sympathetic studio engineer, Paul 'Groucho' Smykle. Before us he had worked with Linton Kwesi Johnson and Black Uhuru. He was Island Records in-house engineer.

We did not have any industry interference. We just handed over the album with completed artwork to the record company and they did their thing, although we were aware that the only reason we could be like that was that we had Mick Jones (ex-Clash) involved and could start halfway up the ladder. Mick had a lot of clout.

I took a cinematic approach to songwriting, hence the script-type lyrics and samples. When we played live my keyboard had coloured stickers on the keys to show me what to do. That's punk rock! As I had no formal training as a musician, I came up with ideas that weren't necessarily musical, but definitely highly original. I kept that Orson Welles statement "if you want to make an original film, don't watch movies" at the front of my mind, and applied it to lyric writing.

Our first single "The Bottom Line" was a track that Mick had put together during his last days with the Clash, and was originally called "Trans Cash Free Pay One". It combined hip-hop beats with a guitar riff and was released in 1985. We shot the video for "The Bottom Line" in Trafalgar Square in London. Obviously there were loads of people there, even more than usual because there was also a political protest going on. The organisers came over to tell us that we were messing up their protest and I told them, "Fuck off, we are making a video." Which looking back on it was not a very right-on thing to say—especially since it was an anti-apartheid rally.

Due to our contacts our name got about quickly. Rick Rubin and Russell Simmons had been on the scene since the Club Negril days in New York and had gone on to form Def Jam Records, which was more sample and drum machine-based than the live instrumentation of Sugarhill Records. Rick Rubin had always wanted to work with Mick Jones, and expressed an interest in Big Audio Dynamite. The Beastie Boys themselves had been huge Clash fans as was Chuck D of Public Enemy. Pretty swiftly a remix of the "The Bottom Line" was released on Rick Rubin's Def Jam label. That was bit of a coup back in those days.

Soon after we finished recording what became the first B.A.D. album, Joe Strummer turned up at Mick Jones' flat totally out of the blue. Mick and Trish went to Nassau a few days later staying at Chris Blackwell's place. Joe turned up on a bicycle with a Tesco's bag to see Mick again. He wanted to get the Clash back together, but Big Audio Dynamite was now Mick's thing.

Our first album, *This Is Big Audio Dynamite*, was released in late 1985. Some have said that floating within its grooves is the album that the Clash should have followed *Combat Rock* with. Much has been written about *Cut the Crap* in a negative way, but there's some good stuff on there. Well, I like "This is England" anyway; it highlights everything that was great about Joe Strummer's songwriting. In my opinion when Mick left the Clash, the band ended.

On *This Is Big Audio Dynamite*, "A Party" was about apartheid and "Stone Thames" was written about Aids. The song title was a take on Rock Hudson. The track "Bad" was one of the first tracks we did together. "E=MC^2" was influenced by the films of one of my favourite directors, Nicholas Roeg. I sampled dialogue from *Performance*, *Walkabout*, *The Man Who Fell to Earth*, *Eureka* and *Bad Timing*. Nic Roeg's son Luc directed the video and we incorporated clips from his dad's films. "E=MC^2" became a chart hit, which must have been a big deal for Mick after his time with the Clash. We played on *Top of the Pops*, it was Mick's first time as well as ours.

"Medicine Show" took a dig at media manipulation and I sampled dialogue from *A Fistful of Dollars*, *The Treasure of the Sierra Madre*, *A Fistful of Dynamite*, and of course *The Good, The Bad and The Ugly*. The advertising campaign for the single borrowed Eli Wallach's killer line from *The Good, The Bad and the Ugly*, "One bastard goes in, another bastard comes out". The video (co-directed by Kevin Hewitt) was a visual counterpart to the themes explored in the song and featured cameo appearances from Joe Strummer, Paul Simonon and John Lydon.

Before Mick and Joe finally made up whilst working with us on *No. 10 Upping Street*, they had a kind of formal get-together on the set of "Medicine Show". We had Joe and Paul playing cops, and there is that poignant shot at the end of the video where Mick is in prison and Joe and Paul are looking at him.

On the day of the shoot John Lydon had drunk a whole case of beer and for whatever reason he and Chris Salewicz got into a fight. I think it was something Chris had written about John in the music press a few years previously.

We used blank-firing machine-guns in the video and John shot the still photographer at point blank range. Fucked him up. We also hired a De Lorean car for the shoot and we had great plans for it until the guy told us it would cost extra to drive it, so we ended up pushing the car from behind with us framed just out of shot. So the car slowly crawled into shot— totally against the grain for a De Lorean—we wanted it to screech in with rubber burning.

The new album was promoted with a short tour of the UK in November 1985, and after a one-off date at the start of 1986 we flew out to play two dates in the USA. I remember some kid in the audience in the US kept repeatedly shouting for us to play "London Calling", and he got booted out of the gig by about twenty people. B.A.D. never played any Clash songs as it was not Mick's thing.

B.A.D. was a huge success live. US college radio stations were really into us, but the record company did not quite know where to place us. The gigs came thick and fast. We played three nights at the Brixton Academy in London, eleven nights at the Irving Plaza in New York and seven nights at the Roxy in LA. I remember we came off stage after one of the nights at the Plaza, when we got to the dressing room someone said, "Bowie wants to meet you."

I replied, "Where is he then?"

The guy pointed to a door in the corner of the dressing room like a broom cupboard and said, "He is in there."

Bowie had been sitting in this tiny little broom cupboard waiting for us to get dressed after we had finished on stage—and out of the broom cupboard he came! I think it was that same night at the Irving Plaza I looked around our dressing room to see Peter Frampton, Dave Stewart, David Bowie, Jimmy Cliff, Mick Jagger, the Beastie Boys, and Paul Simonon.

Touring was a steep learning curve for a non-musician like me. In the early days when we first played live, I had to sample the parts for the upcoming song while I was on stage before we kicked each track off, as I was using the most basic sampler ever invented with very little storage space. Eventually I got an Akai sampler that saved all that grief. I still had coloured stickers on the keyboard. Dan Donovan spent about five years trying to show me where Middle C was on the keyboard. And I never did manage to find it. Also, since day one, Greg, B.A.D's drummer played along to a drum machine. In 1985 nobody did that—he did not even have an earpiece to keep him playing in time either.

Sometimes our enthusiasm got the better of us. Mick wanted every tour be an event, so we'd end up having up to five bands supporting us on the road. On various tours we had people like LL Cool J, the London Posse, Paul Simonon's Havana 3am and Schooly D. Schooly's beatbox was so big that once we had to buy it a seat on a plane. B.A.D. carried on the Clash's tradition of making the line-up culturally interesting. Add to the mix Raymond Jordan (security), Flea (Mick's guitar tech), Josh Cheuse (art department), Guy (merchandise) and my brother Desmond as road manager. Basically all the ingredients for a mobile disaster and the most amusing of times. Financial suicide but one hell of a ride.

When B.A.D. toured Ireland, Leo and I got attacked. We were staying at some shitty hotel, and when we first checked in we had to walk through the bar. It was like the pub scene in *American Werewolf in London*. The bar went silent and people just stared at us. The vibe was not good. Later that evening some guys came out of their room drunk, saw Leo and I in the corridor and totally freaked out. They started attacking us, well an extremely drunk Irish version of 'trying to attack'. Leo grabbed a fire extinguisher and sprayed them trying to dampen the situation. Maybe seeing two dreadlocked black men for the first time had freaked them out. Whenever we went through customs, it was always Leo and I that were given a hard time, so the others used to make sure that we went ahead first on our own, otherwise the whole band would get turned over.

When we were in New York recording our second album, *No. 10 Upping Street*, I bumped into Joe Strummer in Times Square and invited him down to the studio. Joe eventually set up a bunker underneath the piano in the studio and went on to co-produce the album with Mick. Joe had this amazing infectious energy, so that even if he did not want to take over a project, he just couldn't help it; his enthusiasm and energy put him in that position, which was never intentional on his part. It was great to see Mick and Joe getting on again. Joe co-wrote the songs "Beyond the Pale", "Limbo the Law", "V Thirteen" and the single "Sightsee MC!". Jim Jarmusch directed the video. He was a long time friend of Mick and Joe's and a film-maker we all greatly admire. The a black-and-white film was shot underneath the Westway in west London, where the gypsy encampment is.

I always hated the title *No. 10 Upping Street* which was supposed to be a take on No. 10 Downing Street that nobody got. We had all the ideas for possible names and sleeves for the album plastered all over the studio wall. It was like an art installation, but one morning we came in and it had all gone. The cleaner had thrown them all away.

Interesting people were always dropping into the studio, like Iggy Pop, some of the Red Hot Chili Peppers, Jim Jarmusch, Matt Dillon and Laurence Fishburne. It was also around this time that I met Grace and Jessica (R.I.P). The former would become a significant person in my life but that would be later—sort of.

Joe Strummer got Matt and Laurence to do a bit on one of the tracks "Dial a Hitman" which was about an assassin and a hit that had gone wrong. We had them act out a scene in the studio, a phone call between them where the hitman is given the wrong information and kills the wrong person.

One evening photographer Bob Gruen dropped by with a Thai stripper, as you do. He'd been documenting the Clash from the start and had become a close friend of B.A.D. Bob came with some serious photographic credentials (Lennon,

Zeppelin, Stones). Anyway that night he came with a stripper, who proceeded to throw off all her gear and start dancing round the studio. We were all perfect gentlemen, nobody did anything—except for me, who of course filmed everything.

Recording in New York took around three months surviving on very little money. In fact, we never made that much money with B.A.D. as money did not seem that important to us, well not at that point. What was important was travelling to far-off places and immersing ourselves in different cultures. We didn't slog our guts out with fifty gigs across America, we did residencies and spent the rest of the time hanging out in whichever city we were in. We used the same method as the Clash, albeit somewhat scaled down; we announced a gig in a smallish venue and the demand became so great that we ended up playing many nights in the same venue.

When we finished recording, we previewed *Upping Street* in the penthouse suite of Morgan's Hotel in New York. That turned out to be a highly debauched affair. After all, this was the eighties and I'll put my hands up, I was right there, we all were. All the extremes, excesses and drugs, without the dodgy politics. There were no casualties in the band. We did what we did without going too crazy and we knew when to stop, it was all about whether you were taking the drugs or the drugs were taking you.

No. 10 Upping Street came out in 1986 and because of Joe's input there was more of an emphasis on Mick's guitar. I wrote "C'mon Every Beatbox" with Mick as an anti-racism chant. It sampled dialogue from *The Cotton Club* (Laurence Fishburne again) and *Batman.* and featured a Ramellzee sample.

Someone described the song as "Eddie Cochran meeting Run DMC in McDonald's". The video also had cameos from Neneh Cherry, Andrea Oliver and Sipho (R.I.P) from the London Posse.

At that time we were listening to a lot of Def Jam stuff, especially the Beastie Boys and Public Enemy. We were also huge Prince fans and closed our shows with our version of "1999". The album cover was an homage to the Brian De Palma film *Scarface* that we (and the rest of the hip-hop nation) were all very much enamoured with. We had samples from the film on "Limbo the Law".

I had written a track called "Sambadrone" about a Robin Hood-type drug dealer that lived in the Favelas in Rio The people in Brazil loved that tune, but the powers that be didn't. There is a picture of the Police Chief flushing our record down the toilet on the front of a newspaper—kerching! It was amazing writing a track in a basement in Ladbroke Grove and it touching people thousands of miles away.

When we first went to Brazil, predictably I had to sample the local produce and was not overly impressed, so I sampled some more. Half an hour later we had a press conference; there was B.A.D. all sitting at a table in front of two hundred press guys. After about five minutes I could feel sweat just pouring off me. I looked at Mick and he burst out laughing. We're talking Niagara Falls. Normally I could keep things together, but not this time. I had to leave the room fast. What made it worse was I knew that everyone in the room knew that this limey had overdone it. Shame.

Mick Jones and I went to Jamaica for a break after the release of *No. 10, Upping Street*. I was sitting on the beach at Goldeneye and there was this figure walking towards me. It was Keith Richards with a huge bowie knife. This was *The Pirates of the Caribbean* before they'd even written the script. We struck up a conversation and became friendly. He invited Mick and I back to his place; Tommy Steele's old house. Over the next few weeks we spent many evenings over there. It was kind of surreal because there were massive bugs there and when you hit them with a hammer, if you were that way inclined, they made a horrible squeaking sound. So there's Mick and Keith jamming on guitars, Jack Daniels is in the house, the Rastas beating their drums and some other brethren killing these giant bugs. Hunter S. would have been proud.

During the summer of 1987 we supported U2 on the second leg of their European tour. We went down well with the audience, as they were generally more open than most. Initially it was a buzz for me, as we were playing in front of 100,000 people, but by the end I became a bit blasé about it all. I'd be standing in front of all these people, still not being able to play, and I'd hold up the keyboard to show the audience the stickers on it. One of the reasons I moved around on stage so much was to make myself look busy. I guess supporting U2 was more of a trip for Mick Jones; for him it was like a reminder of what he could have had with the Clash. I remember one night sitting at the back of some huge stadium watching U2 plough through "Bullet the Blue Sky" and Mick and I both looked at each other and did not have to say that much. We were both thinking the same thing.

Before *Zoo TV* took off at the start of the nineties, we had our own *Flintstone* version during the eighties. We had thirty TV sets, or sometimes a single screen on stage that used to play a visual collage. It was essentially a prototype version of what U2 did a few years later.

Basically I used to make visual cut-ups, i.e images nicked off the telly and we had them playing behind us on stage. You know the kind of thing: you're at home, stereo cranked to eleven, you're flicking the TV remote and for an instant picture and music sync. The desired effect was to be captivating and ignorable at the same time Some of the audience phoned up the *NME* to complain about it. Guess it was a clip from *Taxi Driver* or it might have been that razor slashing an eyeball from *Un Chien Andalou*. One fan was so disgusted that he swore to never buy another B.A.D. record—wimp.

In the same year we played at the Free Nelson Mandela/ Anti Apartheid concert at Clapham Common. It was a buzz to play on my home ground of South London. The promoters had the headliners on early in the day, as they had a curfew for the live music to stop and were scared of running out of time with a headliner on stage. So Big Audio Dynamite was the last to play, and it got a bit raucous so the police shut the whole thing down. Maybe they didn't like my samples of gunshots ringing out over south London at that time of night!

Gil Scott-Heron and Boy George were on the bill also. It was at a time when George was going through his slightly troubled phase. He came on stage covered in this white stuff, it looked like he had tried to bake a cake and it had exploded.

In 1987, two youths in Hudsonville, USA were charged with making bombs. Somehow the cops linked movies and music to the actions of the two high school students. The cops raided their houses and took away various items as evidence that somehow included two Big Audio Dynamite albums. Our band name and also the photo on our first album with Mick holding a stick of dynamite had obviously freaked them out. Talk about paranoia.

We struggled financially after *Upping Street* was released, as we had spent the advance on recording the damn thing in New York City. Mick had a studio set up in his basement, so we began getting ideas together there. We started recording what was to become *Tighten Up Volume '88* at Beethoven Studios, a small recording studio in west London that was cheap. We had Bill Price on board who had worked with the Clash. Seal was our tea boy; he was living in a squat and just hung around the studio making us tea all day. Obviously he went on to do bigger and better things.

We also worked on the album at Konk Studios, owned by Ray Davies of the Kinks—we ended up locking him in the toilet by mistake one evening. It was the only time I have ever seen Mick Jones slightly in awe of someone. Ray Davies and the Kinks had been such a huge influence on him.

The album was originally going to be called *Dread Astaire*, but we settled on *Tighten Up Volume '88*. The Trojan *Tighten Up* series had left a big impression on us all, so twenty years later Big Audio Dynamite named their album in honour of those compilations. The album was produced by Mick, and the cover artwork featured Paul Simonon's painting of people of different races and tribes partying in front of west London tower blocks; that really summed up the multicultural vibe of London and B.A.D. If there is an overall theme on *Tighten Up* it is about race.

For "Just Play Music" I sampled sixties pop quiz, *Jukebox Jury* and the voice of sixties pop promoter Larry Parnes. "The Other 99" featured the sampled voice of Richard Attenborough from *Brighton Rock*. "The Battle of All Saints Road" combined samples of *The Battle of New Orleans* with raga-style toasting. "Esquerita" was an ode to American rhythm and blues singer Eskew Reeder (aka S.Q. Reeder). I also sampled a lot of stuff from Indian movies and old Ska albums for one of my personal favourites, "Funny Names".

Mick became seriously ill with pneumonia during the tour for the album, thankfully he recovered, but it took a long time. B.A.D. was inactive for the rest of the year, so I carried on with my film work. Whilst Mick was ill we demoed what was to become our fourth album, *Megatop Phoenix*. When Mick recovered he came in and sprinkled his magic over the tracks.

If our first album was a ganja album, so was *Tighten Up Vol '88*, then *Upping Street* was a cocaine album and *Megatop Phoenix* was an ecstasy album. I hasten to add that this is from my perspective. *Megatop* was far more psychedelic than the previous ones, it sounds like a trip. The second 'Summer of Love' had a huge influence on *Megatop Phoenix*. At the end of the eighties Acid House had a massive impact on youth culture generally. As well as B.A.D., bands like Primal Scream and Happy Mondays were mixing modern dance music with rock'n'roll. The Primal's *Screamadelica* remains an all-time favourite of mine; it really captures the spirit of that era.

B.A.D. had such an open brief we could accommodate whatever we chose within our sound. Mick and Dan were particularly into the rave scene, much more so than me. It was great seeing white kids getting sort of funky.

What was interesting about the scene was that it was informed by punk, the whole concept of making your own records in your bedroom and releasing them yourself. I did not like standing in fields that much, but I did like the no celebrity vibe. Eventually the faceless became the well-known. The rave scene was almost devoid of politics, but there was the crusty element that was very political, manifesting itself in the Poll Tax Riots and Repetitive Beats demonstrations.

However, despite it having good music, not much else came out of the rave scene. It is often said that the only thing the ravers did after coming off the dance floor was recover. It did not have the completeness that punk had; the combination of the film-makers, the writers, the photographers and the rest. Besides Irvine Welsh, I am hard pressed to think of other people who were inspired to do more than dance. But I guess it's a good start. Maybe it is because I am from an older generation, but other than people like Primal Scream, Leftfield, Underworld, The Orb and the Mondays, a lot of the music didn't really touch me. Oh yeah, the Stone Roses were the bollocks.

The first single to be released from *Megatop Phoenix* was "James Brown" which featured sampled bits of dialogue from the man himself. The next single was "Contact" which had The Who sampled on it, and was given the remix treatment by Judge Jules. Another fave of mine, "The Green Lady" was written about the Tretchikoff print that Mick's nan, Stella (R.I.P), had on the wall while he was living in Wilmcote House, a Council tower block in west London. It was nan that also inspired "Everybody Needs a Holiday".

After recording the album, we went to Amsterdam for the opening of MTV Europe. Before we reached the MTV studio we decided to check out some of the local produce. So, we started with spliffs, followed by space cakes, washed down with space yoghurt. By the time we reached the studio and got on stage, we could just about stand up and look at each other. Needless to say, that TV appearance was never broadcast. The track "Free" for the film *Flashback* starring Dennis Hopper and Kiefer Sutherland, was to be the last recording I made with B.A.D.

Big Audio Dynamite was Mick Jones' vision. He was the Damon Albarn of that time. He would never have got away with doing what he was doing in B.A.D. in the confines of the Clash, just like what Damon could not do with Blur and what he went on to do with Gorillaz. Funnily enough, Paul Simonon hooked up with Damon for a new project—The Good, The Bad and The Queen in 2006.

The band started to implode shortly after *Megatop Phoenix*. All the usual cliches and dramas, the creative and financial arguments that most bands go through, well, the bands that I like anyway. I'm suspicious of people that stay together for too long.

It was an honour to have been in a band with Mick Jones, and to have written great songs with him, but even at the end I felt I was still in Joe Strummer's shadow. Joe had always kept the standards so high, I perpetually felt like I was splashing around in the shallows. Also there were topics that, as a black man, I wanted to address in the songs and I could not really expect Mick to sing about those issues. It would not have sounded right. That led to me breaking away and having a go with my own band, Screaming Target (named after the Big Youth album) with Greg and Leo. We also had two female singers (Chezere and Mary) in the band, which was a new angle. Dan and Steve Roberts (R.I.P) joined a few months later. I just wanted to know if I could do it on my own. I guess it was more of an ego exercise than anything else.

We were signed to Island Records and released an album called *Hometown Hi-Fi*. Screaming Target had more of a reggae and world sound than B.A.D., but it lacked the magic of Mick Jones. Chris Blackwell advised me to get a singer for the album. I never did (you were right Chris). Chrissie Hynde featured on a track called "This Town" and Pete Wylie was on a track called "Bedazzled".

Even though we did get some blinding reviews, after a while I got fed up with being in a band altogether. It is a diffi-cult existence, especially when you are trying to do something different. Record companies perceive you as not playing the game. We were not naïve sixteen year-olds, we were grown men and it was hard to put up with a lot of that shit. We were also on the 'scampi circuit', having to travel around in transit vans while touring, as well as sharing hotel rooms—something B.A.D. never had to do. Screaming Target lasted for about a year, then Leo, Greg, Steve and Dan went on to form Dreadzone.

Big Audio Dynamite and Screaming Target have been the only two times in my life where I have stepped out of the shadows. Actually that's not true, while I was in B.A.D. I did star in a movie called *Midnight Breaks* with Robbie Coltrane and Toyah Wilcox. I think I prefer staying in the shadows. So, as I had continued making promos for other bands all the way through my time with B.A.D., after Screaming Target I took the decision to put all my time and energy into film-making.

23

FORWARD TO AFRICA

Another phone call. "Don, do you want to come and cover Namibia's independence?" Namibia had been ruled by South Africa and was getting its independence. Not surprisingly, South Africa had mined everything it could get out of Namibia before this went down and there was nothing left. Namibia borders the South Atlantic Ocean between Angola and South Africa and is about half the size of Alaska. As a country it is prone to drought; there are very few natural water resources and consequently it is the first place in the world to incorporate the protection of the environment into its constitution.

South Africa occupied the German colony of South-West Africa during World War I and administered it until it annexed the territory after World War II. In 1966 the SWAPO guerrilla group started a war of independence for the area that was soon named Namibia. In 1988 South Africa agreed to end its administration in accordance with a UN peace plan for the entire region. Namibia got its independence in 1990 after multi-party elections and a constitution was put in place.

This was the first time I had been to Africa and it was a trip. The first thing that hit me, besides the heat, was: big culture shock. Just getting off the plane and being somewhere where everyone is black was a head fuck. Seeing everything being run by black people—double trip. I was looked on with suspicion as I was with this white film crew and they seemed to be able to relate to the white guys better than they could relate to me. Once again, the black English speaking man with dreadlocks directing white people was confusing for everyone. They had not seen people that looked like me in any position of power.

Through Rastafari there had always been the notion of looking back to Africa which I had taken spiritually rather than literally. When I got to Africa I was shocked to find out how far removed I was from the black African experience. I realised that it was me that was really the lost tribe. With all my so-called civilisation, I was totally out of my depth. I can remember driving out to the bush. We ended up getting lost. Before going into the desert we were supposed to register with the Namibian authorities so if we got into any trouble they knew roughly where we were. But of course we didn't bother registering. We ended up running out of fuel. There was a moment when we thought we were well and truly fucked; it became apparent when humorous banter stopped and everyone sat in desperate silence. We were lucky to be found by a German safari party. I had never been so glad to see white people in my whole life.

There was a tribe called the Himba who were so far removed from civilization they were totally unaware that their country was about to be given back. Actually they were so out of the loop I'm not sure they were aware it had be taken away in the first place. While we were driving across the desert in our Jeep, you could see there was nothing ahead us for a day or more, and you knew there was nothing behind us for days and there'd be these Himba guys walking along the roadside. Where the fuck were they going? At night, even though I was surrounded by the beauty of the African skies, I was totally freaked and praying to see an electric light bulb, as we were completely cut off from civilisation.

I was totally unequipped for this shit—the white guys would be sleeping on the ground and I could not do that. I was thinking about the bugs and insects and whatever else might come and join you in your sleeping bag. It is funny how white guys have no problem about sleeping on the ground—like at the Glastonbury Festival. If it were down to black people Glastonbury wouldn't exist. We've spent our lives trying to get off the ground and into a comfortable bed, you get me?

I remember going into a meat market and the way that they keep their meat in some parts of Africa is that you actually let it go off. When it goes off the top layer goes crusty and protects the inner layer so you eat the middle bit.

I was like, "Yo dude, what is this smell?"

But the locals all said, "What smell?" I could not deal with it and sent the cameraman in to get some shots.

Namibia's independence was a big deal. Thousands of people were filing passed Nelson Mandela and shaking hands—myself included. I remember thinking about how he had the weight of all the people's hopes and dreams on his shoulders and there was no way that he could fulfil them all.

Jesse Jackson turned up for the ceremony and I had my little Super-8 camera and wanted a brief sound bite from him. Jesse broke into an "I am doing a public address and five thousand people are watching me" type speech. I didn't have the balls to tell him that the film had run out. As right-on as his speech was, I was only looking for a little sound bite and five minutes later my arm had gone dead from holding the camera. Ten minutes later and my arm is about to drop off.

When the South African flag came down and the Namibian flag went up it brought a tear to my eye, it was deeply moving. You could feel thousands of years of grief being stripped away, whilst knowing at the same time that the years ahead were not going to be that easy either.

Africa left a big impression on me.

24

BEHIND THE LENS

I have made near enough 400 promo videos in my time. My first was for PiL. They chose me as they did not want to use "boring old farts", and we had a good relationship. The love of bass has that effect. I was interested in working with people, rather than any particular musical field. I've made videos for acts as diverse as the Jungle Brothers, the Pretenders, Aswad, Elvis Costello, Ratt, Baaba Maal, the Slits, Maxi Priest, Musical Youth, Big Audio Dynamite, the Pogues, S'Express, Black Grape, Beenie Man, Deep Forest, Apache Indian, Eddy Grant, Sly and Robbie, Yaz, Linton Kwesi Johnson, George Clinton, Bob Marley and, of course, the Clash.

Obviously there is a story behind each of the promos, and they are too numerous to tell—but I have always (well, nearly always) had a good time directing.

Pretty soon I began to make a name for myself, and as I was the only black video director around for quite some time,

I was the first choice when it came to making the few videos that were commissioned for black artists back then. You have to understand that this was when videos were in their infancy. Initially most were made on virtually no budget, and were the complete antithesis of the Hype Williams type thang (damn that kid's good!).

I have often been lucky to be in the right place at the right time. Once I happened to be hanging around at Island Records when Black Uhuru had just done a photo session. I looked at the set they had built for the shoot and said, "Hang on, if we drag some equipment in, we could make a video." We ended up with a video for "Solidarity" featuring the original line up of Black Uhuru, for under a grand.

Most of my videos have been shot in foreign locations. I like immersing myself in foreign culture. When I was growing up I did not get the chance to leave Britain and explore faraway lands. If the budget was big enough, I was on a plane looking for a palm tree. The world is a big and beautiful place. I did not need to invent an idea, they just needed to be discovered. So I used the video making process to turn myself and others on to new things.

In 1982, fledgling UK reggae band Musical Youth decided to give me a shot. I directed a version of the "Pass The Dutchie" video before Musical Youth even picked up a record deal, so we only spent around two hundred pounds on it. Once they were signed, the video could not be used as it did not comply with union rules, so I re-shot the video with a budget of ten thousand pounds. The new version was technically sharper, but the ideas were still the same.

These kids could actually play their instruments, write their own lyrics (for the most part) and had a really healthy attitude. The record companies had considered black music as a minority thing at that time and did not want to invest money in videos. Hopefully these Musical Youth videos did something to change the industry's attitude.

The song title was taken from a Mighty Diamonds' track called "Pass the Kutchie" as in the herb pipe. Obviously these little Brummie kids could not be singing songs about weed. So they decided to find something that rhymed with kutchie. In Jamaica there is a thing they use to cook food in called a dutchie, so the song became "pass the dutchie" which made the lyrics nonsensical. I completely ignored the lyrics and came up with a scenario about them skipping school and being taken to court by the truant inspector. The most important part of the video for me was the location. I filmed them on the Southbank opposite the Houses of Parliament. I imagined this video would be shown around the world and people would be expecting to see the stereotypical image of London, but I messed with that preconception. At the start of the song one of the kids sings "this generation rules the nation with version" and you then see them playing in front of the Houses of Parliament and I thought that was showing a new face of London.

But the biggest source of pride for me was my video was the first featuring a black artist to be played on MTV, beating Michael Jackson by several months. "Pass The Dutchie" got to number one in eighteen countries and reached the top 10 in America, eventually selling five million copies. It was even covered on the national newscasts.

When MTV started, their audience was white, middle-America. They did not show any black videos. They did not even play anything that *sounded* black. Naturally there was a big debate about this. It came to the crunch when Columbia and CBS said, "If you do not show Michael Jackson's "Billie Jean" video, then we will pull all our videos". MTV were therefore forced to show "Billie Jean", which was acknowledged as the first black video to be shown on the channel. But people have subsequently told me that "Pass the Dutchie" was actually the first black video to be shown. Maybe it was not classed as being a "black video" as these kids were all little and cute. I guess if you are four-feet high and have a Brummie accent, then you cannot be that threatening.

Pre-"Billie Jean", I got a call from MTV about doing an interview to talk about my Clash videos. I went to the MTV offices and everybody looked at me strangely. I was taken to a little back room and the guy said, "Look Don, I don't know how to tell you this, but we did not know you were black."

In jest, I looked horrified at him and exclaimed, "Oh, my God, I am black! I didn't even know!"

The guy then sheepishly told me that their policy was not to show black videos—or even videos that sound like they could be black. The guy even mentioned an example; Tom Tom Club's "Wordyrappinghood", that featured an animated video (which apparently was OK), but the record itself sounded too black. The guy blamed it on the 'management upstairs' and he assured me that once there was a power shift, things would change. The upshot was that they did not do the interview with me because I am black.

Godley and Creme wisely used automated mannequins for the award-winning video for the single "Rockit", because if Herbie Hancock had appeared in the video, then MTV would not have put it on their playlist. It was a constant pain having racial censorship in those days. Another decision I did not understand occurred when I submitted the video for the Gap Band, and a scene at the end where the singer and a white girl run off into the water was cut completely!

The real irony of the story is how things have changed; a few years later *MTV Raps* (created by Peter Dougherty and Fab Five Freddie) became the biggest programme on MTV ever. Look at it now; the culture has totally turned around, and black music dominates MTV.

After "Pass the Dutchie" was such a huge hit, I took Musical Youth to Jamaica to shoot the "Never Gonna Give You Up" video. It was a major culture shock for the Musical Youth kids when they got there. Life in Jamaica is hard, people see it as sun, sea and sand, but there is also a lot of trouble and strife. Musical Youth were treated with the utmost respect and were seen as being heroes. Now, this shoot was a fucking nightmare. The idea was to have Musical Youth playing on top of a bus in the middle of Kingston, with a cameo appearance from a reggae star who I would rather not name. Anyway, we started filming outside a record shop where the bus was parked. The owner of the record store came running out and demanded that we had to pay him four thousand dollars to film outside his shop and use his power supply. No fucking way! So we struck a deal with another shop further down the road.

We set up again and by now a massive crowd had gathered around the bus and each and every member of that crowd demanded that we paid them for being in the video. Next our cameo star appeared, and demanded three thousand dollars for his appearance in the video. We haggled with him until eventually it became impossible for us to come to an agreement. While all this was going down, I had the cameras rolling and got what footage I could.

Again the Jamaicans on the street did not know what to make of me. It was a surreal sight for them to see the English dread with a film crew of ten white honkies working for him. Everyone was saying, "Don give me a job, Don give me some money." I had to walk around with the pockets of my shorts hanging out to show that I had no money.

There was a famous place called Idlers Rest where all the reggae musicians used to hang out. Many of these reggae artists that people in the UK imagined to be livin' it large, were in reality living hand to mouth. Eighty percent of the reggae musicians that were stars in the UK were broke in Jamaica, which was shocking. It is that old rock'n'roll story where musicians are paid a small amount for their work or contribution to a track, and told to fuck off and then the producer or record company reaps the reward.

While I was shooting some footage on the beach for the Musical Youth video this white guy from the record company approached me and said, "Hey Don, I hope there is not going to be too many black people in this video!" I was fucking furious and I pinned the guy to a tree. He did not want too many black people in the video, but what are Musical Youth?

So, they had another top ten hit and then the record company decided that they did not like the direction I was taking, and wanted to clean them up. They said that I was making them anti-establishment, but that's what everybody liked. I was doing other film work, so I was not too bothered, but did feel sorry for the kids. The next video had them in short-sleeved shirts and Panama hats, a sort of colonial stylee. The group was finished after that. Not that I am saying that it was because I did not work with them, but the record company just sent them down this other road. Sometimes you crossover and you can't get black. Musical Youth got totally fucked by the experience, all that money in such a short time, family wrangles, some of the guys are actually dead now. Man, what a mess.

During the eighties I was being represented by Limelight, a London-based company of some repute, who had just opened offices in Hollywood. So the dread ends up spending six months living in the Sunset Marquee whilst directing for them. Now Hollywood really is Holly*wierd*. How else would yours truly end up eating pizza with Jack Nicholson, flying down to Utah in the Osmond's private jet or being chatted up by Lauren Hutton? Limelight got me to do a video for the bass player Tyron Brunson which featured an up-and-coming youngster known to you as Ice-T.

Next up was an American heavy metal band called Ratt, who not only *looked* like Spinal Tap, they actually *outdid* Spinal Tap. Imagine me trying to pull that one off. Hey, I need to eat and pay my rent like the rest of y'all! I brought into play the psychology I had learnt whilst working in clothes shops. Making people feel at ease, so that they can relate to you, is part-and-parcel of video and film-making. When I met these guys they were dressed in spandex with long hair and glitter. I managed to connect with these dudes and pulled off a really good video. Subsequently they went on tour supporting Mötley Crüe. When the video came out, it did so well that Mötley Crüe ended up supporting them!

Milton Berle played himself and a woman in the video. He was old-school Hollywood, a Dame Edna sort of guy who was actually related to one of the band members. At the same time Mel Brooks was in the studio next to me working on his *History of the World* film. I have a picture of Mel dressed as Hitler, Milton Berle dressed as a woman and myself—somewhere.

I then did the promo for "Party Train" by the Gap Band which was massive in America. This soul and funk band from Oklahoma had infectious hits like "Oops, Up Side Your Head" and "You Dropped A Bomb On Me". These guys were so out of it when they arrived on set all they could do was walk twenty yards along Santa Monica beach two times and that was it. One of them bit the make-up girl on the arse.

For the following video I flew down to Jamaica for Eddy Grant's "War Party". Eddy had moved to London from the West Indies during the sixties and topped the UK singles chart as a member of the Equals with "Black Skinned Blue Eyed Boys". Years later the Clash covered an Equals track called "Police On My Back" on *Sandinista!*.

During the eighties the art of video making was finding its feet. My stuff was always a bit more rough-and-ready compared to the other end of the scale; the more glossy stuff like Duran Duran's "Rio" video. Despite that, I am not knocking the "Rio" video, as it was typical of that period and a good representation of a direction I definitely did not want to go in. I was always the rebel guy on the fringes. Whilst "Rio" was going on, the brothers were working out the next step, and about to kick everyone in the arse with hip-hop.

I was asked to do one for the Psychedelic Furs' "Sister Europe". the first single from their debut album released in early 1980. The Furs singer, Richard Butler and his two brothers, Tim and Simon, had seen the Sex Pistols and the Clash at the 100 Club. They were inspired to start a band. The Psychedelic Furs were not a second rate punk act. Roxy Music, David Bowie, Velvet Underground and the New York Dolls shaped their early sound. At the start of the shoot, the Furs' singer Richard Butler came up to me and said, "What should we do, look mean and stare at the camera, or should we roll around like we just don't care?" I swiftly replied, "Hold on dude, you are the band. I am the film-maker and you are supposed to know how you should come across." That episode was a sign of things to come.

In the current climate if you are not good looking and you can't dance then you are fucked—whether you can write your own songs or not doesn't even come into it. I'm not trying to sound like a grumpy old man here, but I come from a generation that listened to John Peel or Radio Luxembourg late at night on a transistor radio with a flaky signal coming and going. The emphasis was not on the image but the music. Choreographers and stylists did not run things.

The Happy Mondays had split up in 1992 and three years later Shaun Ryder returned with more mayhem mixing funk with house and rave in a way that was not dissimilar to Big Audio Dynamite.

Black Grape! Where do I start with those guys? I got involved with them through their management, who had also worked with Big Audio Dynamite. We shot the video for "Reverend Black Grape" in Manchester. I remember one scene where Shaun Ryder is dressed as a preacher dancing with two Bunny Girls. We were shooting and Shaun waved his arms at us and said, "Wait a minute." He leaned over and threw up, as he had just done some smack round the back. He wiped the spew off his face and gave us the signal to start rolling again and ended the song without stopping.

I ended up taking Black Grape to Jamaica to shoot the promo for "In the Name of the Father". On the way there the plane nearly got diverted as Shaun got into a fight with one of the air hostesses. But they landed in Jamaica and I went to the airport to collect them. Before they even got out of the airport, these guys had managed to score drugs. So we got to the hotel and there was a knock at my door. It was Shaun.

"Don't tell the others, because we made a pact that we were not going to do crack any more. Can I borrow your bathroom?"

I said, "Sure Shaun," and he was in there sparking up.

After he left there was another knock on my door, it was Kermit.

"We have made a pact that we would not do crack."

"Sure, go and use my bathroom."

This carried on for about four or five days. I can remember another time when Shaun was feeling quite hyper on the set and I had some Valium with me because I hate flying. I gave him the four pills that I had and he chucked the whole lot down his neck. It has to be said he managed to perform very well after that.

A lot of people are better on these things than off them. When they are off them or trying to find them they are a fucking nightmare. Give them the shit and they can get on with the work. The promo ended up being great. As fucked up as some of these guys seemed to be, there was also an admirable quality to them. Black Grape did not give a fuck about how their behaviour or videos would affect their record sales, and naturally, their debut album went straight into the charts at number one.

I remember shooting a video for The Heads, which were half of the Talking Heads (Chris Franz and Tina Weymouth) with Shaun Ryder on vocals. Shot in a tranny bar, Shaun was so out of it that he could not remember the words so we had to hold up a prompt board with the lyrics on behind the camera.

I come from a time when it was all about standing for something, as opposed to falling for anything, and there is a lot of that going on these days. It is hard to find people with an attitude like Shaun Ryder these days, as everyone is scared of having an opinion or upsetting anyone.

The same can be said for Shane McGowan. When I shot the Pogues video for a track called "Summer in Siam", I had to write two scripts. One if Shane McGowan turned up, and the other if he did not. I had known Shane from the days of the Roxy when he was in his band the Nipple Erectors and there was a bit of mutual respect. Shane turned up for the shoot and we propped him up on a tea chest, did about two takes and he was off. It was a great looking video with a Thai concept and a host of Thai boxers.

For Jimmy Cliff's "Reggae Nights" I wanted to shoot on yet another beach in Jamaica (plane tickets and palm trees), but it was full of tourists. So, I ended up shouting, "You'll have to leave the water, there is a shark in the area," and there was widespread panic. The hotel staff came out and threatened to beat me up as all the tourists left the beach in a hurry and didn't return for a week. Working with Jimmy was a trip—after all, he was the star of *The Harder They Come*. And naturally there are no sharks in Jamaica—not in the sea anyway...

I also shot a video in Jamaica for the legendary drummer Lowell Dunbar and bass player Robert Shakespeare, known as Sly and Robbie, who had worked with Peter Tosh, Black Uhuru, Grace Jones and Mick Jagger to name a few. Sly and Robbie were working with American hip-hop act Boogie Down Productions and what was more interesting than the video shoot itself, was the fact that we were bringing these hip-hop dudes from New York to Jamaica. Yet another culture clash.

These guys had been used to going to Miami for their holidays and coming to Jamaica was a shock for them. You would think that there would be some similarities between both cultures, but in reality there was a huge gap between the two. These guys were standing on the beach in their big leather puffa jackets and they wanted to go for a piss, so I told them to go and find a bush. They looked aghast and wanted to find a toilet. Even my white film crew pissed behind bushes and ate the food in Jamaica, while the black Americans wanted to find a McDonald's.

On the other hand, the Jamaican guys in the video had been watching too much MTV and were trying to talk like the Americans. The natural comedy of the whole experience inspired me to write a script called "More Fire" (written with Chris Salewicz) about black Americans going to Jamaica and the culture confusion.

I did a few videos working with Apache Indian, the big one being "Boom Shack-A-Lak". His material was a combination of Asian and Jamaican culture, similar to my ancestry. My roots are Jamaican, both my parents were born in Jamaica but my mother's parents are both from India. Apache had grown up in Handsworth, Birmingham, which was where Steel Pulse came from. Apache initially got involved with reggae sound systems, but by the end of the eighties he had become known as a "Dancehall rapper" and cut his first single "Movie Over India" in 1990. He soon signed to Island Records and released tracks with a more political edge like "Movin' On", a rallying cry against the electing of a BNP candidate in Tower Hamlets.

I took Apache to Jamaica and in return he took me to India. That was a buzz. The first things that overwhelmed me were the heat, the smell and the poverty, especially in a city like Bombay. When I left the hotel there were thousands of fans on the street waiting to see Apache. I had people tugging on my dreads begging me to give them money. The first week I was there I gave them everything I had, but after a couple of weeks of being constantly hassled my patience ran out and it's like, "Look, fuck off, I've no more to give".

I shot videos for Baaba Maal in Jamaica and in Africa where I collapsed on the set, nearly died. I did not drink the water but it was the ice cubes that got me. Where we shot the video was beyond a one-horse town. Baaba had the only car in the entire village, which only had one bar and one shop. I say *had* the only car because while we were there it got wrecked in a collision with a donkey. One day I remember a Dunhill cigarette rep turned up selling cigarettes in this one horse no donkey town in the middle of Africa—just what they needed.

The current industry does not want someone like me trying to push my agenda, or any agenda, other than flogging records. After all the record companies are not there to enlighten the people, their job is to keep people stupid and take their money. I have to do work that inspires and moves me.

Music videos started to go pear-shaped when as well as pleasing the artist, you had to placate their manager, the marketing people, the record company and MTV. In the early days the video makers were in control. Later it became video making by committee. There is that saying "what is a camel?" and the answer is "it is a horse designed by a committee" which says a lot for what happened to video making. It all got messy when record companies started to bring in stylists and choreographers telling the bands what they should look like, how they should perform. If a stylist has to tell a band what they should look like then they are not a proper fucking band. If you do not know what you are about then you ain't supposed to be there.

I never tried to please everybody, if 70% of people liked it, then I had won. The other 30% was down to taste, lucky I got some. If it pleased everybody then there was something wrong with it. When I made videos for the Clash, the band liked them, I liked them and we were away. OK, videos always were about selling the record, but if you are smart enough you can convey some good ideas as well.

The corporate politics of pop video-making soon got the better of me. I opted for making documentaries, as record companies did not want me and I did not want them. I guess the final straw came around the time I did a promo for a friend of mine's band called Johnny Boy. The record was called "You are the Generation that Bought More Shoes and You Get What You Deserve". It is a great record—great title! I can remember sitting in the editing room with the band, the manager, the A&R man and the publicity guy, basically people from six different departments, and thinking this was ridiculous.

❋   ❋   ❋

The beginnings of my life as a documentary film-maker can be traced back to the start of the eighties when I went to Jamaica at the request of Chris Blackwell, who I had established a relationship with a few years previously. He was in the middle of producing a film called *Countryman*, a reggae movie about a Rasta maverick, with Bob Marley, Steel Pulse and Wally Badarou on the soundtrack. Co-written and directed by Dickie Jobson, it was the highest-grossing Jamaican film when it was released. It is the story of a fisherman called Countryman, whose lonely existence is shattered when an airplane crashes into a nearby swamp. By rescuing two young Americans from the wreckage, Countryman becomes an unwitting player in a political plot devised by the power-hungry Colonel Sinclair. The rescued couple and Countryman, branded by Sinclair as enemy agents, are forced to flee into the Jamaican wilderness where Countryman shows the Americans his knowledge of the land and sea.

Chris Blackwell decided to get me to shoot Black Uhuru and Toots and the Maytals playing live to maximise the fact that he already had the film crew in Jamaica. It gave me the opportunity to experiment with filming in a more documentary format, not limited to the short, sharp editing that was demanded by music videos. For me, one of the most interesting things about the whole episode was I got to hang with Michael Rose, Duckie Simpson and Puma (RIP), the original line up of Black Uhuru. We went back to their yard and spent a long time 'reasoning' about Rastafari and they interrogated me about what the hell I was about. I was sitting with them in this ghetto yard and I guess I had this romanticised view of it all. They saw it for what it was—a slum yard—and I'm like, "But, this is roots reggae." Somewhere lying in Blackwell's vaults is some great footage of Michael Rose and Duckie Simpson chanting "Rastafari" and licking the chalice as they disappear in massive clouds of smoke.

Looking back, it was these really privileged moments that I almost took for granted. Black Uhuru's first album was a major inspiration to us in the UK as far as black identity was concerned. There was a lot of heavy Rasta philosophy to it, which gave us in the UK a positive angle on being rebels.

For the same project I spent some time travelling with Frederick Hibbert, better known as Toots of the Maytals. Unbelievable fucking geezer. I had been listening to his records since my Dad used to play them in his sound system. The Maytals were the biggest group in Jamaica during the sixties and first recorded as Ska artists at Coxsone Dodd's Studio One in 1962. Toots' vocal style was often compared to Otis Redding. His *Funky Kingston* album from 1975 was one of the few Jamaican records that helped introduce the white rock audience to reggae music.

Toots was a follower of the Coptic Church, that had been set up by some white American hippy types in Jamaica. They had this headquarters, a sort of red, gold and green spaceship-type building in the mountains that I visited with Toots. The white hippy Americans were apparently using the church as some kind of front to fly weed to and from Miami. They were very clever about it, and subsidised all these things that they thought the local people would benefit from. For a little while, they captured the imagination of many of the Jamaican locals.

I can remember a trip to the Coptic Church with Toots driving down these winding roads at 100 miles per hour. I was shitting myself. Mind you, this is the same guy that when I asked, "What side of the road do you drive on in Jamaica?" he replied, "Cha, just drive man, just drive."

Chris Blackwell was also the man who instigated the idea of starting a reggae film archive. Steve Barrow, Rick Elgood and myself were all involved. Steve had begun working with reggae when he started Daddy Kool, London's premiere reggae shop during the seventies, which sold more than two thousand different reggae records in 1976 alone. Steve now runs Blood and Fire, a highly respected reggae and dub re-issue label that is highly rated for the quality of the sleeve design, sleeve notes and previously deleted or hard to find records like *Pick A Dub* and *Heart of the Congos*.

As many of the reggae pioneers were getting on a bit, Chris Blackwell decided it would be good to get their story first-hand rather than through some white academic twenty years after they died. Chris appointed Carl Bradshaw of *The Harder They Come* fame as our co-ordinator. It was a privilege to work with this guy. Every project that I have worked on in Jamaica has involved Carl in some capacity, and probably would not have happened without his help. He had played the wide boy in *The Harder They Come*, a character called Jose. It is quite funny, when you drive around Jamaica with him, even to this very day you will hear people hailing him up, shouting out "Jose, Jose". The thing is, he really is that character. Carl really epitomises the spirit of Jamaica.

For the reggae archive he went around documenting all the reggae pioneers and I filmed around a hundred people. Amongst many, I captured Prince Buster, John Holt, Tappa Zukie, Yabby-U, Derrick Morgan, I-Roy (RIP), Ken Boothe, Jah Stitch, Bunny Lee, Prince Jammy and Delroy Wilson (RIP). We managed to get King Stitt and Count Machucki (RIP), two of the very first DJ's, to talk about the early days of Studio One. It was fun sitting and listening to these old boys, they had incredible stories to tell and within those stories are the cultural and social development of Jamaica itself.

Blackwell also got us to go down to Black Ark, Lee Perry's famous studio. This was after Lee burned the studio down—all that was left was just the shell of the building. I can remember Lee bending down to say "hello" to a banana plant and talking to various trees. People say he is crazy, but when it comes down to business, he is 100% sane. I think most of the time he is working his whole "Salvador Dali of sound" image. A few years later I directed a documentary for Island Records called *Return of the Super Ape*. It was a brief profile of Lee's life. He turned up for that interview in an Indian head dress!

Through these projects and doing various videos for Chris Blackwell, our relationship has continued over the years. I worked on a long-form video for him called *Legend*, about Bob Marley. It was really a re-edit of archive material featuring live footage and interviews interspersed with all the Bob Marley videos that I had directed after his death. *Legend* was massive.

Chris Blackwell was also the one that got me to west London. I'd been moaning about living in Hollywood and coming back to live in a council flat in Brixton. He scrawled something on a paper napkin (again!) and told me to go see one of his people. Next thing I know I'm living in Ladbroke Grove with a foot on the property ladder. Thank you C.B.

Planet Rock

In 1996, the BBC made a ten-part series on the history of contemporary music called *Dancing on the Street*. It was their most expensive commitment to a music series with a budget of five million. I was asked to direct the last episode called *Planet Rock*. The documentary focussed on hip-hop and the effect of black music in the eighties. A brave move on the part of the BBC and especially for their partners, WGBH out of Boston. I returned to New York to film artists like Africa Bambaataa, Grandmaster Flash, Chuck D, De La Soul, Run DMC, Beastie Boys, Arthur Baker, Chicago's Frankie Knuckles and the Detroit legend Derrick May. Those were the days—my camera vehicle was a white limousine (cheap as taxis back then) and we had the budget for helicopter and crane shots. The premise of my episode was how black music gave new life to the dying carcass that was rock'n' roll. No shit!

Westway to the World

The Clash had talked about doing a film over the years but Joe, Paul and Mick had not thought that the time was right. For some reason, everyone agreed that this was the time. I knew that there was a great story waiting to be told on film and I knew that eventually I'd get the call because of our history. I also had a lot of previous unseen footage of the Clash. Even the Clash did not know that the stuff existed. There was footage from live shows and the Clash rehearsing in '76, TV shows and news footage.

One thing I loved about the Clash was that their songs were about something. Joe Strummer's lyrics—any two of his rhyming couplets had more content than most people's fucking albums. What the Clash could do in three minutes with a song was a fucking trip. Strummer constantly moved the lyrical goalposts of what rock music could deal with. It is said that if the Pistols made you want to smash your head against the wall, the Clash would give you a reason. You don't get bands like the Clash any more. They were a tough act to follow, more like damn near impossible!

Good music documentaries reflect the time and capture the era in which they were made. I really wanted to do that with *Westway to the World*. I didn't want to do the usual *MTV Rockumentary* or *South Bank Show*-style documentary where the director or producer puts their slant on the story. Doing this film with them made me think that they were all born to be in the Clash, their roles in the making of this film reflected perfectly the roles each of them had in the band. *Westway* is the story of the Clash, not the Clash MK II. The band that I knew about included Mick Jones. I concentrated on primarily using just interviews with the band for the film. I knew what lines I could and couldn't cross with them, and I knew how far I could push as well. Despite that, nothing was off limits and if they did not want to answer a question they just didn't.

Having a voice-over was not necessary. Most bands have problems stringing a couple of sentences together, but the Clash didn't have that problem. I have always done the interviews for my documentaries myself in the past, but as I knew the Clash so well, this time round a writer called Mal Peachey did them. If you talk to someone you know well and they realise that you know the answer to the question, they only give you half of the answer.

Mick was into every single damn detail. He was interviewed for about three hours. Once we were done he said he wanted to do it again. I said, "What, the last question?" and he replied, "Nah the whole thing". Mick had come in for the interview and was a little anxious. He was always regarded as the bad guy in the Clash, but it really was not that straightforward. So, Mick was on the defensive and on the first interview he came off as being reserved. We shot the interview again. Joe was also interviewed for three hours and spent two of those discussing his life before the Clash—the relationship he had with his father and his brother—which he had never really talked about that much before. I got the distinct feeling that, although he knew I couldn't use a lot of it, he wanted to get it off his chest. I have just given it to film-maker Julien Temple, who is making a full-length feature about Joe Strummer. So people will get to see it anyway.

In *Westway*, all the black and white studio footage came from Julien. He had got behind a camera at very much the same time I did. He had some early footage of the Clash that I did not have and I had some footage of the Sex Pistols that he wanted for *The Filth and the Fury* so we helped each other out.

Topper was hardly in *Westway to the World*, but the few moments he is in it he is frightfully honest. "I'd like to apologise to them for letting the side down, for going off the rails, but if it happened again, I'd probably do the same thing," he says, and I admire him for that. I always thought of him as being like Frankie Machine in Nelson Algren's *The Man with the Golden Arm*. Joe was generally disinterested, and Paul wanted to make sure that everything was in the spirit of the Clash style.

People often say to me, "Why didn't the Clash continue?" But I think part of being a great band is knowing when to stop. Longevity was never the point, but their legacy is timeless. I was awarded a Grammy for *Westway to the World*. I like to think that the Grammy was actually for Joe Strummer, as he had sadly passed away a few months before. It is not why any of us got into doing our stuff anyway, to get awards. My brethren in Brixton thought it was cool though.

I wanted *Westway to the World* to be a rock'n'roll blueprint, to show people other ways of getting somewhere like the Clash did with their music and I did with my film-making. If people don't have examples to inspire them then what are they going to do? All they see today is *Pop Idol* and bloodclaat *X-Factor*!

For the extras on the *Westway* DVD I managed to salvage 30 minutes of *Clash on Broadway*. It takes you back to early eighties New York, before zero tolerance, Starbucks and the Gap dominated the streets. The city you see in the film is bursting with energy, unbearable heat, cops, seediness, garbage, yellow cabs, B-Boys on street corners and Hispanics going about their business, graff-covered walls and subways. Think *Taxi Driver* crossed with *Warriors* and you are close. Along with images of the Clash exploring New York, they are shown in their dressing room preparing to take the stage to Ennio Morricone's "60 Seconds to Watch". Once they hit the stage, the crowd goes wild as they launch into their explosive set of songs that draw heavily from *Sandinista!* and *London Calling*. It is as much a film about New York as it is the Clash conquering it.

I did approach Bernard Rhodes for *Westway*, but he declined to get involved. For what reason I will never know. Bernard is really a law unto himself. From my perspective, that was stupid Bernard!

After I won the Grammy, I did not have any work for six months. It was strange, the school of thought is that you get a Grammy and then get loads of offers, but what really happens is that people tend to think that you are too expensive to work with.

In 2003, *The Essential Clash*, a compilation DVD was released featuring all the videos that I directed for the band, and a few I didn't. There is also the trailer for the *Clash on Broadway* movie and the interview that the band did for the *London Weekend Show* in '76. More importantly Joe Strummer's *Hell W10* film was also included. It was something that Joe directed in west London during January and February 1983 as a side project in between touring and recording. This guy just never stopped, his energy was as endless as it was infectious. Joe was the kind of character who could say, "Go and jump off a cliff" and people would. Except for me—I would be filming it.

Strummer had this knack of making everyone feel that they were special (even though in many cases they weren't) or that they had a role to play in the big picture. He could rally people together with his enthusiasm and for *Hell W10* he did just that. Nobody got paid for being in the film and it involved many long nights; I think it is a great testament and a good example of the persona of Joe Strummer. It was a silent black and white film that had Paul Simonon playing a character called Earl, and Mick Jones playing an underworld gangster called Socrates. Both characters were at war over a consignment of heroin. After Joe finished the film he forgot about it.

The story of how it ended up on the DVD is really bizarre. Years earlier some guy picked up a VHS copy of it at a car boot sale and gave it to me. It was a cutting copy of the original film and as far as we know it is the only copy that exists. I put a soundtrack to the film with some obscure unreleased Clash instrumentals. I did not want to do much cleaning up of the film. It is rough and ready which suits the style of it, but without a doubt the vibe cuts through. Mick Jones is particularly funny hamming it up as a villain.

For the 25th anniversary of *London Calling*, I made *The Last Testament* (which was the original title for *London Calling*) Clash consigliere, Kosmo Vinyl, who for whatever reason also did not appear in *Westway to the World*, told the story of the making of the album. There is some amazing old footage of the Clash in Wessex Studios with legendary producer Guy Stevens, whose technique included pouring wine in pianos and smashing chairs in the studio while the Clash are trying to lay down tracks.

I still miss Joe—we all do. Mick, Paul and I remain good friends to this day. Simonon is one of the most solid geezers you could ever meet and as cool as fuck.

Dancehall Queen

In 1998, Chris Blackwell started Palm Pictures with the aim of releasing innovative music and film projects and *Dancehall Queen* was the first film they released. I had always thought my first film would be London-based. In fact I've just finished a script to put this in motion called *Don't Touch That Dial*. It is centred around the story of a pirate radio DJ who after being falsely accused of murder is forced to go on the run. He has to use what he's got to get what he needs and uses the pirate radio to plead his case. Predictably music is integral to the narrative. I guess it's a kind of homage to *The Harder They Come*. Bertolucci once said that we all only have one good idea and we spend the rest of our lives re-interpreting it.

So, Jamaica it was. Chris Blackwell was setting up a DVD label and *Dancehall Queen* was going to launch it. I spent three months rewriting the original script with Suzanne Fenn (it was co-directed by Rick Elgood). I am immensely proud of the film. For me, as a black British man of Jamaican ancestry, to get the thumbs up from the people of Jamaica was moving. When the film was shown in Jamaica there were riots in the street, in the same way there had been for *The Harder They Come*. The Cineplex was rammed, there were three people trying to fit in one seat. *Men In Black* was showing at the same time, and *Dancehall Queen* did so well there that they had to take *Men In Black* off.

Dancehall Queen is *The Harder They Come* from a female perspective. It is about a girl called Marcia (Audrey Ried), a humble street vendor who through the world of dancehall escapes to a better life. Call it Cinderella without Prince Charming coming to the rescue—Marcia created her own luck. From my point of view it was the women of Jamaica that were making all the social changes. All the guys just want to be Ivan from *The Harder They Come*. Marcia has ambition and the drive to achieve it. The film concentrated on one example of this with the dancehall, but there are also Jamaican women getting into the academia to help build the infrastructure of the country much more so than men. Jamaica recently elected its first female Prime Minister, and that's a big deal. She can't do worse than the men have done previously, that's for sure.

Trying to shoot a film in the middle of Kingston was like a cross between working in Notting Hill Carnival and a war zone, and I am surprised we managed to pull it off and make the film. Also it was shot on mini-DV, which was a major feat in those days, and if memory serves me well, pre-dates the whole school of Dogma thing. The cameraman was Louis Mulvey who I've worked with on most of my films and respect is due. One big advantage of shooting the film digitally was that as the cameras are so tiny no one took them seriously and because of that, they would open up. Also, the bigger the camera, the bigger the bill. It helped us get beneath the surface; shooting digitally got us through a lot of doors.

When we were doing the night time shoots, there were dogs barking all over town. Once one started, then they all started. Carl Bradshaw told me, "There is two options, either feed dem or shoot dem."

I remember giving out some scripts to the guys during rehearsals and once they'd got them they disappeared and would not come back. I was trying to work out what was going on. Then it dawned on me that they could not read. Little things that I took for granted really struck home. Working with people like Beenie Man was also a bit of a test. When those guys turned up on the set something that should have taken half an hour took half the night. He'd be somewhat distracted by his entourage, and by Carleen, the real Dancehall Queen—not to mention 'nuff herbs. But despite that, his undeniable charisma brought something to the whole story. Lady Saw also featured in the film. She's like Jamaica's Millie Jackson using her sexuality to get her point across. She scared the shit out of me.

When I first saw *The Harder They Come*, there were certain lines of dialogue that really struck a chord with us, like "Who's a bad man? One bad man come out an' draw", which became "samples" in our culture before we even knew what samples were. I wanted to do the same thing with *Dancehall Queen*. In the film there is a scene where the bad man Priest is threatening some potential witnesses, and he says, "Walk and live, talk and bomboclaat dead". I wrote that as a sample and sure enough, it became one. Talking to young Jamaicans today, when you mention *Dancehall Queen*, "Walk and live…" is the first thing they recite back to you.

Dancehall Queen was premiered in Brixton—now that was a huge buzz! My parents came to the screening, as did friends from back in the day. What made it even more poignant for me was that it all took place at the very cinema where I had seen *The Harder They Come* back in the early seventies, and here was *Dancehall Queen* shown in the same building. Back in my teens it was called the Classic, known locally as the "fleapit". Now it is called The Brixton Ritzy and somewhat more gentrified—no dirty old men sitting at the back any more.

When Chris Blackwell decided that he wanted to make *Dancehall Queen*, he wanted to only use Jamaican actors. He did not want to fly any English or American stars in, as he did not want the film watered down for the world market. Other than *The Harder They Come*, most Jamaican films had diluted the culture. It was a very brave move for Blackwell. It was just as empowering for Jamaicans to see a true representation of themselves on screen as it had been for me to see Jimmy Cliff in *The Harder They Come*.

Chris Blackwell had the vision to help create a Jamaican film industry, so in that vein another film was commissioned called *Third World Cop*. It was directed by Chris Browne and the script written by Chris Salewicz and Suzanne Fenn. In 2003 Rick and I were approached to do a film called *One Love*, which is described as a "feel good" film. I had a few problems with the "feel good" aspect but it looks fantastic, which is all down to Rick Elgood. It is really Rick's film, as *Dancehall Queen* is mine. On the set of *One Love* I was responsible for working with the cast, a mixture of first-timers and pros to get the best results. It starred Ky-mani Marley and Cherinne Anderson. She was cast for *One Love* because of her riveting performance (her first) in *Dancehall Queen* and because I remembered that she use to sing whilst waiting for her takes on set. A diamond in the rough. The film took an old-fashioned solution to a modern problem. Whilst I can appreciate what the film was trying to say, I thought the idea dated. But it cannot be denied that Jamaica does need a lot of "feel good".

During the filming, one of the most interesting aspects for me was to witness the changes in Jamaican society since I first went there back in the seventies with John Lydon. For example, ganja was the drug of choice back then. At the time of filming *Dancehall Queen*, there was a lot more cocaine and crack coming into the mix.

For me, the most obvious change came to Jamaica during the early eighties when the emphasis shifted from live music to studio-based recorded music. In Jamaica, the term "Dancehall" has been used since the fifties and that is literally what it meant. Over the years the meaning of the word shifted several times and became associated with a specific incarnation of reggae. It has always been the cultural climate and changes in technology that have influenced the changes in reggae.

At the end of the seventies, independent producers like Henry 'Junjo' Lawes used the Roots Radics as a backing group for sessions at Channel One. What came from that was Barrington Levy's *Bounty Hunter* album, engineered by the Scientist, which is a good example of taking reggae in a new direction. There was also Wayne Smith's hit song "Under Mi

Sleng Teng' from 1985 which heralded a further change. I liked it as it was still in conjunction with the organic sound of a reggae bass line. But more recently the emphasis moved to the kick drum rather than the bass line. With technology advancing during the eighties with cheapish keyboards using built-in sounds, all you had to do was to hit a preset button and boom, the tune was there—not.

It didn't help that most of the new artists had no musical grounding in the first place. In a weird way, whilst technology has freed up most people around the world, it seems to me it has almost fucked Jamaican music. There is a downside to affordable technology—mediocrity. I always thought it was a combination of the organic and the technological that made things more interesting.

In many ways, ragga was a backlash by those who had not reaped the rewards from reggae's international success. Soon most of the lyrics would be about bravado and violence. No longer were political themes being addressed. Also, the Kingston drug trade had strong connections with New York, Miami and Washington, and crack and cocaine were now the drugs of choice. This shift in Jamaican culture can be heard in the music.

A lot of music coming out of Jamaica today is culturally bankrupt. I learned a lot about my own heritage directly through reggae music at a time when it was about something. Nowadays there is the odd guy saying something (get VC's "By His Deeds") but for the most part we're talking sexist, homophobic, gun-glorifying shit. Anything that makes you think twice about what you're actually doing falls by the wayside.

Much of today's ragga music is made for the moment, not for longevity, and something to be heard in the environment of the dancehall. With Bob Marley, Jamaica got cultural respect around the planet and now Jamaica has lost that global appeal and ragga seems to mostly appeal to 'the yoots' in the middle of urban cities. Black Americans have picked up on aspects of reggae and ragga; you can clearly hear it within R&B and hip-hop and they have gone one better. It is blind emulation of the American blueprint and the wrong drugs that has sent Jamaican music off on the wrong road. But one thing you should never do is underestimate Jamaica's ability to come back from the brink with a fresh take on whatever it's reflecting. What is needed is more self interpretation. Having said all this is strange to see how a tiny island that has spent years under colonialism has now culturally colonised the planet.

Jamaica is very much a dichotomy—on one hand you have the whole Rastafari roots spirituality conscious thing and on the other side there is a kind of rude bwoy raggamuffin bad boy element. It is that dynamic that makes the place seem so interesting. For some Jamaica is a paradise, for others a pair of dice.

I should add that it was during this period I got busted 'for playing away'. Actually I was working really hard, but nevertheless falling foul of a classic cliché I caused some pain and for that I'm truly sorry.

Gil Scott-Heron

During my formative years, when we were running around like headless chickens desperately trying to find out where we fitted into society, it was people like Gil Scott-Heron who gave us the cultural signposts we needed. I have always been interested in music with an agenda that can inspire, inform and push things forward.

Gil's landmark track "The Revolution Will Not Be Televised", a merging of his highly charged political poetry with a laid-back soul/funk groove, is rightly credited as being the at very the root of hip-hop. His influence has been immeasurable to me, and black culture across the world. In the eighties he even collaborated with Stevie Wonder on his successful bid to have Martin Luther King's birthday made a national holiday—another highly controversial black political statement. Sadly by the nineties his career was in decline and he'd developed a drug problem. In 2001 he was arrested and sentenced to three years for possession of cocaine. It was perceived as a tragically ironic fate for an artist who had preached vehemently against drugs.

In the film Gil is very honest about his problems. It's quite interesting that the people we got to contribute to the documentary tried to romanticise his struggle. One of them even suggested he was "suffering for his art." And he counters, "Look, I'm not suffering for my art, I'm suffering for some shit that I took." Gil's more realistic about his situation than anyone else is. One can have faults and yet still create great stuff. For me, it makes them more real. It's like Strummer: nice guy, loved him to pieces but he could be difficult too. It almost seems to be one of the dynamics of being creative, that nice people don't come up with interesting ideas.

Whilst working on the documentary, the relationship between Gil and myself was strained but it wasn't personal.

As Public Enemy's Chuck D puts it in the film, "He's trying to keep it together whilst the whole time having this fucking gorilla on his back."

At the start of the two-and-a-half weeks we were in New York, I said to Gil, "By the time this has finished you're going to hate my guts". Within about a week he was hanging up the phone on me—something which no-one has ever done to me in my life! But I wasn't going to let the superficiality of what he was going through cloud my view of what he'd done in the past. This guy put out an album and two books by the time he was nineteen in a climate where there was almost no black cultural back-up at all.

Gil turned up for the interview two-and-a-half days late. As I said before, I usually like to make my problems my assets, but he pushed it to the last degree. One thing about Gil is he seems amazingly resilient, although having said that the man looks like a car crash. But Gil Scott-Heron is a soldier. He once described his records as "survival kits on wax; instructional pieces on how to move things forward and make things better." I told him that "I'd like this film to be a survival kit on celluloid." It features contributions from Mos Def and Ritchie Havens, the Last Poets, Linton Kwesi Johnson and Clive Davis.

I would like to think that this documentary will re-introduce Gil to the MTV generation. A lot of the current hip-hop generation does not understand the tradition that they are following in. Gil is one of the building blocks of what hip-hop is all about.

Sun Ra: Brother From Another Planet

On the strength of the Gil film I got to do one on Sun Ra. The only track I really knew of Sun Ra's was "Space is the Place". I was aware of his persona. He is to jazz what Lee Perry is to reggae.

The minute that doing a Sun Ra documentary was mentioned to me, I thought, "He's a black man that broke new ground, I'm there." Whether I like the music or not is totally fucking irrelevant.

I gravitate towards anybody black that breaks out of the confines of what black is. People that are trying to push the envelope, like George Clinton, Sun Ra (RIP), Prince, Jimi Hendrix (RIP), Sly Stone and Arthur Lee (RIP) who all stood out from the pack. They are not defined by their colour. I like to think that I'm the same. People say "Don Letts is black, how did he get involved with punk?" I got involved because I could relate, black ain't nothing to do with it.

Sun Ra broke the traditionalism of jazz by bringing in electric keyboards, synthesisers and embracing the Moog. Everyone was asking "what the fuck are you doing?" and his answer was "jazz is what I say it is." Sun Ra started a record label in 1956, he was doing hand-drawn sleeves and selling records at his gigs during the sixties. This all predated the punk DIY ethic by some twenty-odd years.

For the project I interviewed people like Thurston Moore from Sonic Youth, White Panther leader John Sinclair and Wayne Kramer from the MC5 who had all been inspired by him, and were all subsequently featured in *Punk: Attitude*. The

MC5 and Sun Ra often played gigs together during the early sixties—which on the face of it seems incongruous—spaced-out free-form jazz from another planet, alongside hard-edged Detroit garage rock. John Sinclair saw some kind of idealistic connection between the two bands. But for me it was exactly the same feeling as when I played hardcore dub reggae to the predominantly white punks at the Roxy twenty-odd years further down the line.

The MC5 covered "Starship" and respected Ra. They thought he was beyond civil authority and religion. Wayne Kramer and John Sinclair were happy to give their opinions in the documentary and remain Sun Ra fans—in fact when the reformed MC5 played London's South Bank a couple of years ago, they brought the Sun Ra Arkestra (now being led by Marshall Allen) to accompany them on the bill.

I used footage from a previous documentary called *Sun Ra: A Joyful Noise* and a film from the early 70s, *Space is the Place*. In the film, Ra and his Arkestra land on a planet and go about bringing black people to it. When *Space is the Place* was made, it was fashionable for black music to be located in the ghetto. Sun Ra understood that ghettos are by definition places you want to get out of, not places you want to get into. Ra had to put up with segregation in Alabama when he was growing up. He believed that black people should leave Earth and go somewhere else for a better life.

After listening to all the Sun Ra albums I could lay my hands on (there are fucking hundreds of them!) whilst researching this documentary, I realised that most of his music was going right over my head. Sun cosmology; numerology; and whatever 'ology' he could lay his hands on inspired Ra's music. Even Marshall Allen, his saxophonist for over thirty years, admitted that he "didn't quite get it." But to Ra it was deep and meaningful. He mixed electronic sounds with jazz, long before Miles Davis did. Funny, I just cannot escape punk rock, and as far as I am concerned, that is exactly what Sun-Ra was.

Punk:Attitude

In 2005, some thirty years after the first stirrings of the UK Punk movement, I was approached to make: *Punk:Attitude*. The film was to take me back to where I started and brings the story full circle. I originally had reservations about doing it, but I thought to myself, why do we keep returning to punk and why does it still capture people's imaginations? After all, we are talking about something that happened thirty years ago. Do you realise that we're as far from punk rock now as it was from the Second World War? There have been a lot of movements and subcultures since then, and whilst many have been informed by punk, none seems to have had the same impact.

Punk rock spawned photographers, graphic artists, writers, and people like myself. You do not have anniversaries of other movements every five or ten years, none has had the gravitas. Not that there should not *be* punk anniversaries— that totally misses the point, but it does speak volumes about the impact punk has had.

What we're really talking about here is counter-culture as an ongoing dynamic. It occurred to me that there is an over-emphasis on the late '70s punk incarnation that undermined the bigger idea. People tend to look back on this weird thing that happened in 1977 with Mohawks and safety pins— which it was never about. That was just a media contrivance. I approached the film with the idea of showing it in context; i.e. that it didn't start with punk rock and it doesn't end with punk rock. Furthermore if it happened before, it can happen again, and looking around today it sure needs to.

If I'd have gone to people like David Johansen, Siouxie Sioux or Tommy Ramone and said, "Look I want to do a nostalgic documentary on punk rock", they would have probably told me to take a running jump. What I did was present my story of punk as an ongoing dynamic that started way back, been here for thousands of years. It is about an attitude that doesn't only exist in music. In fact most of the music produced today is probably the last place you'll find it.

For instance, look back at art, poetry and film-making. The literature of someone like Albert Camus, the Surrealist Movement, the films of Buñuel and the comedy of Lenny Bruce are all punk. In the original edit of the film, I wanted to include the example of Marcel Duchamp who was associated with the Dada and Surrealism movements. He shocked the art establishment in 1917 when he exhibited a sculpture called "Fountain", which was a urinal that he signed under the pseudonym of "R Mutt". In 2004, this piece of art was voted the most influential artwork of the 20th century. One of the producers asked me what band Marcel Duchamp was in!

I obviously had to spotlight the Ramones, the Sex Pistols and the Clash, but what I tried to do was give airtime to people that hadn't been given airtime before. The Pistols came from somewhere. The Clash came out of something; they didn't just come out of a void.

Translated to today's culture, the important idea is that you can empower yourself and be individual. There was life before *Big Brother*. I have two teenage kids and I can see them on the edge of becoming just another fan, so I wanted to show that punk was not something to look back on, but something to look forward to, if you are brave enough and you have a good idea. Punk was not about watching, it was about getting off your arse, getting involved and doing something.

Punk:Attitude was quite a difficult project to work on, as it was a co-production between a UK and a US-based company. It was like trying to make a movie about World War II with the English and Germans as your clients. I had to find a way to get round that problem, so I worked towards "*a* truth", instead of "*my* truth". There were a few people I would have liked to have spoken to. Iggy Pop particularly, although he was working on another documentary at the same time. Patti Smith was on tour, and I would have liked to have spoken to Lenny Kaye as we are quite good friends. As for Lou Reed, well Lou is Lou, we will leave it at that. But the idea behind *Punk:Attitude* was bigger than any single contributor. It was never meant to be an A to Z of punk anyway. In fact, the original version of *Punk:Attitude* was three hours long, which was edited down to ninety minutes for the release.

Strangely enough in 2001 I was in N.Y.C making a film called *Downtown to World's End* looking at the early New York movement. Amongst others I interviewed Richard Lloyd (Television), Jayne County and Lenny Kaye. But that project was never completed as three days into filming 9/11 happened.

One of the major problems I had was the cost of acquiring archive footage. In one instance twenty seconds for nearly £10,000. In most cases the money is not even going to the group, and the TV company that has the footage does not even know that they have it until I asked them for it. I wanted to show an example of surreal art and some other company refused permission. I was trying to introduce the movement to a new audience, trying to turn people onto something. Which all poses the question, "Who owns the culture anyway?"

Courtney Love really pissed me off. She refused to let me use any Nirvana music or footage. She took offence to something that Legs McNeill said in the film that was about the business, not Nirvana. I wanted Nirvana to appear in the film as a peak or a narrative arc. Arsehole! How can someone so thick be responsible for something so important?

When I was making the film, I never worried about how it would be received. I never do that. I worry about how I receive these things and the rest is a bonus. *Punk:Attitude* seemed to strike a chord. I spent nearly a year promoting it at various film festivals around the world. It was almost like punk *Groundhog Day*. It was beginning to drive me bloody mad. It was weird going out there and pontificating about something that really is instinctive and intuitive. And the minute you try to vocalise it, it becomes ridiculous. You end up talking about something that you should be doing.

And then there is always that idiot in the Q&A that says, "Why weren't this group or that group in it?" What can you do?

Looking back to when I started we were just young people doing our thing. It wasn't like I was sitting with the great Joe Strummer that people have come to know now. At the time, it wasn't that big a deal. We were just young people trying to do something. That's the spirit I wanted to capture with *Punk: Attitude*.

Whilst making the film I got re-acquainted with some old friends and introduced to some new ones. Henry Rollins is awesome, John Sinclair—you d'man! Strummer (even though he'd passed away) was a huge inspiration; when I was making the film, it felt like he was sitting on my shoulder whispering "Shut up and get on with it". I dedicated *Punk:Attitude* to Joe.

AFTERWORD

At the beginning of 2006 I was off filming Franz Ferdinand in South America. They were supporting U2 and did their own shows in Rio, Chile and Argentina. My last few films have been very controlled stylistically so it was a great opportunity to return to my punk roots. I've found it increasingly difficult to relate to the current crop of bands, the downside of a generation raised on MTV. Most of what's happening today is about as deep as make-up. But these guys have got it going on, you'd have to with a name like that.

Immediately after that I was back in familiar territory. I got another call—did I want to direct a film on George Clinton? Hell yeah. Once again here's someone that ticks all the required boxes for me to get fired up. I'd grown up listening to Funkadelic (well trying to) and busting moves on the dancefloor to the Parliament catalogue. It featured contributions from Macy Gray and Outkast's Andre 3000. Between tracks like 'Free Your Mind and Your Ass Will Follow' and 'Atomic Dog' George always had his finger on the button—ask Dr. Dre. Would you believe this brother was born in a toilet! Talk about funk.

I still want to paint a new portrait of London on film— every city should have a great movie (as well as a great song).

I want to celebrate the cultural mix, the juxtaposition of old and new, the very duality of my existence. I want to reflect on the input we as immigrants have made as I believe that it is this influx that has put the Great back in Britain. Hanging on to an island mentality does not get us anywhere. It's the creativity that comes out of the multicultural mix that makes London swing.

At the end of 2006 I was on the road documenting the birth of The Good, The Bad and The Queen project and filmed their debut at the Tabernacle in west London. This 'Dickensian' dub combo: Damon Albarn (Blur/Gorillaz), Paul Simonon (the Clash), Simon Tong (Verve) and Tony Allen (Fela Kuti's drummer) have created an album shaped by this city that's got my fan 'juices' flowing (truth be told I never really lost 'em). A classic London record, it subtly reflects the mix that rocks our mutual boat with Damon's voice putting a quintessential English stamp on it. It couldn't have been made anywhere else. It's the perfect soundtrack to the movie that is London. Pure technicolor!

Music still gets me out of bed, and on the strength of the music compilations I've released over the last few years I'm DJ'ing both here and abroad again. It's my way of networking and keeping an ear to the ground (no input—no output). I'm still playing a dub reggae-based selection from across the last fifty years. The history and legacy of Jamaican bass culture. It's very much in the spirit of what I was doing during my days at the Roxy—using my culture to turn people on. Last year for example I was in Tokyo DJ'ing for Stussy's 25th anniversary (respect Michael Koppelman and Shin). Someone once told

me that music doesn't effect change, it only reflects change.
Try telling the youths in Tokyo that.

I come from a generation whose soundtrack helped
empower the listener, helped people to be all they could be
and revelled in individuality. I'm living proof that music has
that potential. Today many of these ideas have been lost as we
increasingly become passive consumers, slaves to the rhythm
who are emotionally detached from the planet. There used
to be an element of manipulation on the part of the record
companies and media, but nowadays it seems like there's a
strange complicity. When I was starting out, music was an
anti-establishment thing. Now people get into music to be
part of the establishment. I mean how radical can you be if
you want what the man's offering? It's all about new values.

The current cultural climate feels as if punk never happened. Warhol's fifteen minutes of fame has become a nightmare of people that can't justify three. During the punk days
we used to say never trust anyone over thirty, nowadays I
sometimes think never trust anyone under thirty! For the
most part Western culture has become increasing conserva-
tive, if not darn right stagnant.

Nevertheless I remain optimistic. The punk spirit is
like the force in *Star Wars*—you can't stop it. There's always
something going on, you just got to look in new places and
like Strummer said, 'Make sure your bullshit detector is
finely tuned'. Look to the amateur and the naïve for the new
ideas in the future, everyone else is reading from the same
book. Punk attitude still serves me on a day-to-day basis. As
I've said all along, a good idea attempted is still better that a

bad idea perfected and I'm still turning my problems into my assets.

By the end of this year I will have seen fifty summers. I guess I should be both older and wiser, but I think I got screwed on the wiser part. What I have learnt is that the evolution of mankind is painfully slow. This I know by looking at myself. You look around the bubble that you're living in and you might think otherwise, then you turn on the news (did I mention I watch the news religiously?) and it is a reality check. But when I think of what my parents achieved in their lifetime and the selfless sacrifices they made to set us up, I'm pleased with my part in the process. I've learned that for the most part we have to work towards goals we probably will not live to see. That kind of sucks, but the small changes I see in my bubble get me through the day.

When I was initially approached with the idea of putting my story down, I didn't get it—in a way I still don't. Sure I've made a few cool moves, but I haven't saved anybody's life, nor have I changed the world. I just can't help thinking that what is really required these days are big bold steps to shake things up. I mean you can think what you like, but in the morning you do what you do and that's where it all goes pear-shaped.

Beavering away over the years I've managed to remain pretty much earthbound, collecting almost a full set of life's clichés on the way. I would have like to have said more about the women in my life but that ain't cool and the gentleman in me prevents it. Needless to say they have been a large part of my life and the creative process too. I'll never forget.

I'm now married to Grace with two daughters, Honor who is five years old and Liberty who is just one. Fortunately age and finance prevents Justice! Jet and Amber from my previous relationship are now twenty-one and fifteen respectively. It's interesting seeing the world through their eyes. I have seen some major cultural shifts in my lifetime and on the face of it this should make their journey easier. I sure hope so. Many of the struggles I went through as a first generation British black seem won. But the truth is that they haven't gone away, just relocated, the names and places have just been changed to persecute the innocent.

I'm currently directing the third part of a series for the BBC called *Soul Britannia*. Now this particular film has a strange 'synchronicity' with the closing of this book. Starting with the arrival of the Jamaican immigrants in the fifties, it looks at the impact of black music from that time till this and the social and cultural impact that has followed in its wake. It has really driven home and touched on many of the themes running through my journey and our part in creating a new British identity. However we should be aware of new stereotypes. I mean Sir Trevor McDonald, Moira Stuart O.B.E. and Ainsley Harrriot are black too for Christ's sake. And whilst every one might wanna be 'Huggy Bear' they probably wouldn't want to trade places with Rodney King or Steven Lawrence (RIP). For my episode I roped in people like Jazzie B, Norman Jay M.B.E, Omar, Daddy G (Massive Attack), Beverley Knight M.B.E, Rebel MC, Amy Winehouse, Goldie, Skinny Man, Roots Manuva, Mica Paris and Rodney P. These artists are all proof that the cultural exchange was very much a two-way street. They have had as much impact on Britain as Britain has on them.

On the 25th of March, 1807, exactly 200 years ago, the Abolition of the Slave Trade Bill was passed by the British parliament. So I guess I'm free, relatively. Any bondage I suffer is now primarily mental and of my own making. But what we've gained on the roundabout we've lost on the swing. The sad reality is that, as things stand these days, in my neck of the woods I'm just as likely to be shot by a 'bredrin' as anyone else. It's funny growing up during the seventies I knew exactly who and what Babylon was, but today I ain't so sure. It's a crucial question—just who is Babylon?

As for any wisdom I could impart, forget about it, if the truth be told don't know what the fuck's going on. But what you gonna do, throw the towel in? No way!

I mean someone's gotta keep the fire burning....

I GET BY WITH...

A little help from: Grace, Liberty, Honor, Amber & Jet Letts / Leo Williams / Desmond Coy / Norman Letts / Ashley Letts / Naomi Crowest / Audrey De La Peyre / Jeannette Lee & Gareth Sager / Mick Jones / Dan Donovan / Jim Jarmusch & Sarah / Paul & Tricia Simonon / Chrissie Hynde / Louis Mulvey / Chris Blackwell / Mary Vincent R.I.P / Suzette Newman / Denise Mills R.I.P / Michael Koppelman, Shin Okishima & the Stussy Tribe / Tomo / Bob Gruen & Elizabeth / Fred Rubio & Dierdre / Peter Dougherty & Claire / Gerb / Josh Cheuse & Cara Seymour / John Lydon & Nora / Constantine / Gerry Harrington / Nigel House & Rough Trade / Ari Up / Beth Orton / Sarah Crowest / Scarlett Crawford / Chris Salewicz & Pam / Caroline Coon / Melle Agace / Niel, Perry, Sid & Georgia / Marylyn Dwyer / Davo / Lolly / Bibs / Arthur Baker / Jez Nelson / Jeff Barrett & the Heavenly Crew / James Lebon & Monie / Rick Elgood / Youth / Andrea Oliver / Alison Dore / Anthony Genn / Alan Parker / Adele / Apache Indian / Andrew Czezowski & Sue Carrington / Alan McGee / Adrian Boot / Alex Kaprianos / Robert Elms / Phil Jupitus / Jarvis Cocker / Steve Mackey / Ashley Beadle / Graham Day / Nora Nona / Bobbie Gillespie / Di & Will / Bill Peters / Dolly & Mischa / Laura & Craig / Big Youth / Ben Watt / Bernard Rhodes / Bill Lynch / Beastie Boys / Bez / Chuck D / Mark, Greg & Darnel / Steve Roberts / Cherine Anderson / David & Gwen / Chris Needs / Caroline Baker / Carl Bradshaw / Chris Sullivan / Connie Jude / David Rodigan / Tiina Laakkonen / Daddy G / Denes Ujvari & Celia / David Nobakht / Viv Albertine / Vivien Goldman / Wendy James / DJ Spooky / Duncan Western / Dr. Alimantado / Jessica Stoessel RIP / Dennis Bovell / Debbie Ronane / Dick Odell / Dennis Driscoll / Damon Albarn / Ian Brown / Daisy Lawrence / Dave Hallbery / Dickie Jobson / Futura 2000 / Finola Dwyer / Fab 5 Freddy / Roy 'Froggy' Freeland / Gary Stonage / Gina Pascal / Gabby Salter / Geoff Travis / Greg & Daniel / Michael Schmidt / Joe & Serena / Gigi / Gaz Mayall / Gaylene Martin / Dorothy & Annabelle / Hugo / Haze / Hardy Blechman / Humphrey 'JR' Murray / Helen Storey / Jeremy Marre / Jonathan K. Saul / John Gray / Jazzie B / Jon Savage / Julian & Amanda Temple / Jane Ashley / Shiela Rock / Steven Mills / Simon Fields / Steve Miller / Sharon Scott / Sam Bully / Shaun Ryder / Simon Price / Robin Modiano / Robin Derrick / John Krevine / Jamie & Dave / Jerry Dammers / Jo Faul / Jo Allen / Patti Smith / Mica Paris / Rodney P / Jimmy Auth / Karen Malluk & Phil Schuster / Kate Simon / Haroun / Ira Lippy / Guy Gillam / Kevin Hewitt / Karen Gabay / Kirsten Willey / Kiki Miyaki / Linton Kwesi Johnson / Lauren Jones / Flea & Lisa / Lucy Fawcett / Luc Vergier & Donna / Lee Perry / Mark Cooper / Mark Moore / Mick Barton / Malcolm McClaren / Lucinda Mellor / Lenny Kaye / Liddy & John / Kate Simon / Mick Calvert / Steve Barrow / Russell Simmons / Robert Fox / Michael White / Mikey Cheruti / Mark Zermati / Martin Baker / Rick Rubin / Emma Harris / Robbie Knouse / Spike Lee / Sam Harman / Steve Chivers / Shaun Ryder / Thurston Moore / Tricky / Tessa Pollit / Tony Thompson / Toby, Peter & Praise / Tim & Sarah Bran / Zowie / Zephyr / Xenobia / Dominic Watkins / Marrianne Faithfull / Matt Dillon / Marek Kanieska / Neneh Cherry / Nils Stevenson R.I.P / Nick & Gloria / Ned / David McAlmont / Pete Kalhan / Pearl Harbour / Paul 'Groucho' Smykle / Pete Wylie / Marion Smyth / Pennie Smith / Patti Palladin / Peter Ashdown RIP / Angie Bowie / Paul Cooke / Phil Fisk / Raymond Jordan / Sue Cameron / Siobhan Barron / Steph Raynor / Lydia Latham / Tina Berry / Glenda King / Roz Riens / Joe Dwyer / James Maycock / James Du Cann / Jeffrey Love / John Osbourne / Jo Anne-Scott / Alex Paterson / Tappa Zukie

INDEX

saf publishing

www.safpublishing.co.uk

info@safpublishing.co.uk